HANDMADE GRAPHICS

For more excellent books and resources for
designers, visit www.fwbookstore.com.

13 12 11 10 09   5 4 3 2 1

Distributed in Canada by Fraser Direct
100 Armstrong Avenue
Georgetown, Ontario, Canada L7G 5S4
Tel: (905) 877-4411

Library of Congress Cataloging-in-Publication Data

ISBN: 978-1-60061-800-0

Layout by Anna Wray
Art Director Tony Seddon

media   Front cover art by Gluekit

HANDMADE GRAPHICS

Tools and Techniques Beyond the Mouse

Anna Wray

HOW BOOKS

Cincinnati, Ohio
www.howdesign.com

Contents

From the mid-1980s onward, the Apple Mac grew in popularity as a creative tool for designers, illustrators, and artists. No previous computer had the software to enable such sophisticated graphic and image manipulation. Design studios and publishers stopped using traditional manual cut-and-paste methods, and started using QuarkXPress, Illustrator, and Photoshop. Macs were installed in art schools across the world and creative practitioners started using the software and its possibilities for producing artwork.

Computers and the software package that has now become the Adobe Creative Suite have undeniable benefits. The same results that were once created by hand can be achieved at a much quicker pace and with less manual equipment and space. With the magic "undo" button a designer can create an unlimited number of versions without committing to a final design.

Computers have become an integral part of our daily lives. Owning a PC or Mac with a broadband connection is the norm. E-mail, cell phones, digital television, and Nintendo Wiis are a huge part of popular culture in the Western world.

1

2

1 By Mysterious Al, see pages 32–33.
2 By Kipi Ka Popo, see pages 30–31.
3 By Holly Wales, see pages 18–19.
4 By Jaco Haasbroek, see pages 106–107.
5 By Chen Ying-Tzu (Hazen Chen), see pages 146–147 and 168–171.

3

I could go on championing the benefits of handmade work; however, it would be blinkered of me to simply ignore computers. We can still make use of the benefits of computer technology in the handmade process. We can scan work, tweak it, add to it, and e-mail it—it's never been easier to create a global audience for your work. Computers are useful creative tools, so long as they don't take over the process and limit our creative thinking. Milton Glaser, designer of one of the world's most recognizable and iconic logos, I [HEART] NY, summed up the effects of computers on design perfectly when he said, "Computers are to design as microwaves are to cooking."

This book celebrates and showcases the most innovative contemporary work from international designers, illustrators, and artists whose core practice is to create work by hand. The book is categorized into four main chapters: Drawing and Painting, Printing, 3D, and Mixed-Media Collage. Each chapter also includes step-by-step workthroughs, which reveal a detailed insight into the diverse processes and techniques behind each handmade work.

The purpose of this book is to inspire, inform, and encourage innovation. I hope it makes a welcome and enriching addition to your bookshelf!

4

Computers have a tendency to remove elements of chance, materiality, and texture. The happy accidents that come with experimentation are lost and risk-taking is removed, resulting in images that are highly polished and homogenized. With the digital aesthetic becoming the norm, could it simply be that creatives are growing tired of staring at screens?

Abandoning the Bezier tool and taking up a pencil can be a liberating experience. Drawing is tangible, affordable, and instant; there is no better place to work through ideas than a sketchbook, and why be restricted to a printer for color? There is a huge range of media out there to have fun with, whether it be paint, ink, or felt-tip pens. Each has its own unique qualities and textures, and unlike a printer, the color that you want is the color you get.

Handmade work also has the appeal of being original and idiosyncratic. It frees us from the size restrictions and two-dimensionality of the screen. In this book you will find a variety of creative work made by hand, including wall murals, type, plush toys, and handbound books, to name a few. There is a whole world of creative possibilities out there, and often only the most simple of materials are needed.

5

DRAWING AND PAINTING

This chapter showcases work from a collection of graphic artists and illustrators who use a variety of drawing and painting methods and materials, including pen and ink, felt-tip pens, marker pens, and spray paint, to name a few. Whether it's typographic treatment, mural-based work, paint on canvas, or simple line drawing, all of the artists included in this chapter share similar processes, in that they use a variety of mediums by hand, both traditional and modern, to produce their work.

While every artist has their own personal inspirations and interests, a common thread running through this chapter is the aspiration to create a visual language that is experimental, new, and progressive.

To use one example, Luke Best's illustrations are full of fragmented imagery and narratives. The abstract coexists with the figurative; a woman on a horse is juxtaposed with illegible hand-drawn type. Luke's mix of styles and content is a good example of how artists can free themselves from developing a limited style (see pages 12–13).

This chapter also includes a showcase of hand-drawn typography. There is an increasing movement toward blurring the boundaries between type and illustration, and Jesse Hora is one illustrator working in this style. He has taken a clean, modernist font as a starting point for his workthrough (see pages 45–47), adapting it to form elaborate twists and turns, and then weaving an intricate, linear pattern within the lettering that almost obscures the letters.

Patterns are often employed by graphic artists as compositional devices, used to connect different elements together. This is especially apparent in the work of Rui Tenreiro. In his illustration of physicist Professor Stephen W. Hawking (see page 21),

1

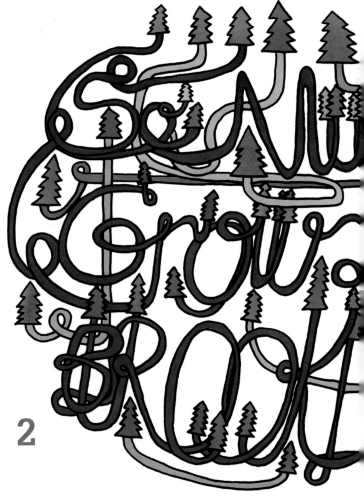

2

4

3

for example, he has woven a complex web of patterns around hand-drawn elements.

David Bradley takes the idea of intricate patternmaking and turns it into something highly conceptual. David draws individual elements by hand using a graphics tablet and then orders the elements intuitively, building together a highly detailed network. The results are enormously detailed, large-scale patterns made from tiny organic elements—reminders of cells—that duplicate and grow into a complex web of life (see pages 36–37).

Another important aspect of this chapter is the influence of street art. The work showcased here has been chosen because of its inventive originality. Rather than drawing on traditional graffiti styles, street art creates a distinct visual language that draws influences from a diverse range of aesthetics. For example, Matt Sewell uses a color palette that draws on a retro 1970s style, while also being influenced by Japanese and fantasy art (see pages 14–15). Matt has provided a tutorial on how to create a unique mural (see pages 42–44).

Federico Martinez Aquino's eclectic wall murals also draw on a range of styles and combine a number of different elements such as people, animals, patterns, type, and shapes, to create a narrative without hierarchy. His murals remind us of the bombardment of visual imagery—an inevitable element of modern life (see page 35).

Finally, one of the most engaging media included in this chapter are felt-tip pens. Felt-tips have many childhood associations, and are often one of the first art materials children experiment with. Holly Wales uses felt-tip pens to create bright and colorful illustrations of retro objects, such as old telephones and typewriters, and her illustrations therefore embody a unique sense of nostalgia (see pages 18–19).

This chapter showcases a diverse and eclectic range of methods and styles, which is reflected in the series of workthroughs included at the end of this chapter— each one offering an insight into the artist's processes. I hope they provide you with the practical and inspirational spark needed to create your own unique drawing and painting work.

1 By Rui Tenreiro. See pages 20–21.
2 By Mike Perry. See pages 28–29.
3 By Jon Burgerman. See pages 24–25.
4 By Holly Wales. See pages 18–19.

Luke Best

Since graduating from the University of Brighton, UK, and the Royal College of Art in London, Luke Best has worked as part of the illustration collective Peepshow and as a teacher at the Camberwell College of Arts in London. His work is inspired by dysfunction, stories, and moments of hesitation and uncertainty. One of Luke's primary interests is to avoid trends, and he strives to create honest work. Luke's aspirations include wanting to make ceramics, knitwear, illustrated books, and to continue developing his drawing skills.

1–2 Pages from the self-published book, We Will All Be Ghosts, *a limited-edition, 16-page, A5-size (5 $^{13}/_{16}$ × 8 $^5/_{16}$in) publication printed on 140gsm recycled paper.*
3 Cover produced with pencil, ink, and paint for On the Edge of Mesa, *a 24-page book limited to a print run of 50 copies.*

1

2

Matt Sewell

Matt Sewell is a London-based artist/illustrator. Matt grew up in the north of England, and his work draws on this rural upbringing, fusing fairy tale-style narratives with bucolic, psychedelic landscapes and a symbolic treatment of animals. Matt's favored mediums have changed throughout the years; his natural style finds itself equally at home on people's feet with his own range of Gravis footwear, on animated adverts for the cell phone network 3, and in British newspapers such as *The Guardian* and *The Observer*. Equally happy using watercolors, spray paint, or acrylics, he has also painted a number of murals and produced a vast amount of personal work, which has seen him gain a large international following.

1 Swan Vistas, *produced as part of a series of 20 individual wooden pieces painted with acrylics.*
2 The House that Jac Built, *a commissioned mural painting in Melbourne, Australia.*
3 *A self-initiated freestyle piece created with spray paint.*

1

2

Paul Willoughby

Paul Willoughby studied at the Loughborough University School of Art and Design, UK. He now divides his time between working from home and his London studio, where he art directs *Little White Lies* magazine (which received the Best Designed Consumer Magazine at the Magazine Design and Journalism awards in 2008) and co-runs The Church Of London Design agency. Paul received his big break as an illustrator when Mickey Gibbons, the art director of (the now defunct) *Adrenalin* magazine happened to pass by his degree show. This led to work for UK newspapers *The Guardian*, *The Independent*, and the *Financial Times*. Paul's favorite drawing tools are Lyra 5B pencils, and his inspiration comes from craft; printmaking; vintage design annuals; oriental design, art, and ephemera; Polish cinema; theater posters; reportage photography; travel; and the Vienna Secession.

1 This illustration for the FT Magazine (published with the Financial Times) relates to ignorance surrounding climate change. The work was sketched with watercolors and a 4B graphite pencil before being composed in Photoshop.
2 This is Paul's graphic interpretation of the Radiohead song, "Nice Dream." It is composed of found graphics and sketchbook drawings scanned into Photoshop, and then screenprinted.
3 This is a personal piece inspired by vintage portraits. Paul cut several postcard-sized pieces of paper from books and drew directly on them with a 4B graphite pencil.
4 This illustration of musician Devendra Banhart was created with a 5B graphite pencil on thick cartridge paper for The Stool Pigeon, a free London music newspaper.

1

2

3

4

Holly Wales

Holly Wales works from her studio in East London, an area well known for its artistic scene, and is also a visiting graphic arts lecturer at the Winchester School of Art in the UK. Her career highlights have so far included creating a large flat artwork for the 2008 Frieze Art Fair in Regents Park, London. Holly explores a variety of subject matter through her self-initiated and commercial work for a range of international clients, and enjoys experimenting with a range of different materials.

1 Polaroid Camera is from a huge collection of over 200 felt-tip pen drawings made for both personal projects and The New York Times Magazine *"Lives" column, published every Sunday.*
2 This illustration was created for a Nestlé annual trend report to promote the concept that nature knows best.
3 Inspired by a conversation Holly overheard in a park, We Do Things *is a series of illustrations produced for Japanese clothing brand Uniqlo's Spring/Summer 2009 T-shirt collection.*

1

2

Rui Tenreiro

Rui Tenreiro's career began in the world of advertising. However, after growing disillusioned he pursued a career as an illustrator and graphic designer, which he found to be much more rewarding. He studied graphic design at Konstfack, University College of Arts, Crafts and Design in Sweden, and works from his studio space in Stockholm. Rui works predominantly in black ink on paper using dip pens, fineliner pens, and brushes, which he then turns into screenprints or textile prints. Rui also runs a small independent publishing company called Soyfriends, which specializes in artist's books.

1–4 All images shown here were hand-drawn for FUKT magazine using fineliner pens.

1

2

3

4

Buff Monster

Buff Monster lives in Hollywood and lists heavy metal music, ice cream, and Japanese culture as his major influences. The color pink, which he sees as a symbol of confidence, individuality, and happiness, is present in everything he creates. He works exclusively on fine art paintings, collectable toys, and select design projects. His art has been exhibited in numerous galleries and published in a long list of books, magazines, and newspapers, including *Juxtapoz Art & Culture Magazine*, *Vapors Magazine*, *Angeleno Magazine*, *XLR8R*, *Los Angeles Times*, and *The New York Times*.

1 Acrylic, silkscreen, and spray paint on a 16 × 16in/40.64 × 40.64cm wood panel.
2 Acrylic paint on a 24 × 24in/70 × 70cm wood panel.
3 Acrylic paint and silkscreen on a 24 × 24in/70 × 70cm wood panel. In this piece, Buff Monster wanted to capture two opposing styles and techniques. It is also seen as a broader statement about opposing forces existing together in harmony.

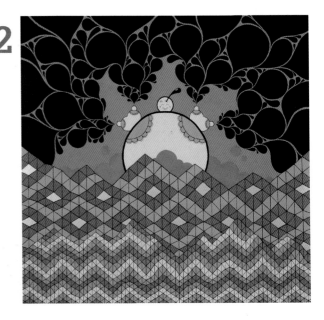

Jon Burgerman

Jon Burgerman studied fine art at Nottingham Trent University, UK. He started his career painting record cover sleeves, which led to further music industry, magazine, and commercial work. Jon's recognizable drawing style combines characters, scrawls, and doodles. He has worked with Kidrobot, Rip Curl, and Size?, made animations for MTV, published a monograph with ROJO (*Gribba Grub*), and produced a host of products available through his own website. His inspirations include other creative work as well as small fluffy animals. His favorite medium to work with is pens, with Biros, Pentel Hybrid Gel Grip pens, Berol felt-tip pens, chunky Sharpies, and Posca pens being his favorites.

1–4 Drawings on recycled envelopes using felt-tip pens, self-initiated for various exhibitions.

1

2

A51400543

3

PRIVATE

If undelivered please return to
PO Box 230
8 Canada Square
London
E14 5RT

UK6703

4

Kenneth Do

Kenneth Do is unusual within the context of this book, as he is mainly self-taught. He lives in Los Angeles, where he works by day in a coffee shop, and by night spends long hours drawing in his favorite medium—pen and ink. He is inspired by animals and everyday interactions with his surrounding environment, including the people, nuances, and music he encounters on a regular basis. His ambitions are to further develop his drawing style, making his illustrations even bigger and better.

1–3 Paper and ink illustrations, each measuring 9 × 12in/22.86 × 30.5cm.
4 In this poster, titled Where did the Magic Go?, *Kenneth wanted to portray how some people lose their imagination as they grow older. It was created by combining an illustration with a photograph of his yard.*

1

2

3

WHERE DID THE MAGIC GO?

Mike Perry

Mike Perry lives and works in Brooklyn, New York. He studied at Minneapolis College of Art and Design in the USA, and has since developed a successful career as a designer, illustrator, and publisher. His first job after graduating from college was as a designer for Urban Outfitters, and after gaining valuable experience he decided to take the freelance route and has never looked back. His work has a strong hand-drawn typographic element, and his favorite drawing tool is the mechanical pencil. Future ambitions include developing products and illustrating installation spaces.

1 ABC Scape, a pencil drawing created as the basis for a screenprinting performance.
2 Save Us, a self-initiated hand-drawn illustration exploring type.
3 Time & Space, an illustrated poem for a client, which propelled Mike to develop a new style of work.

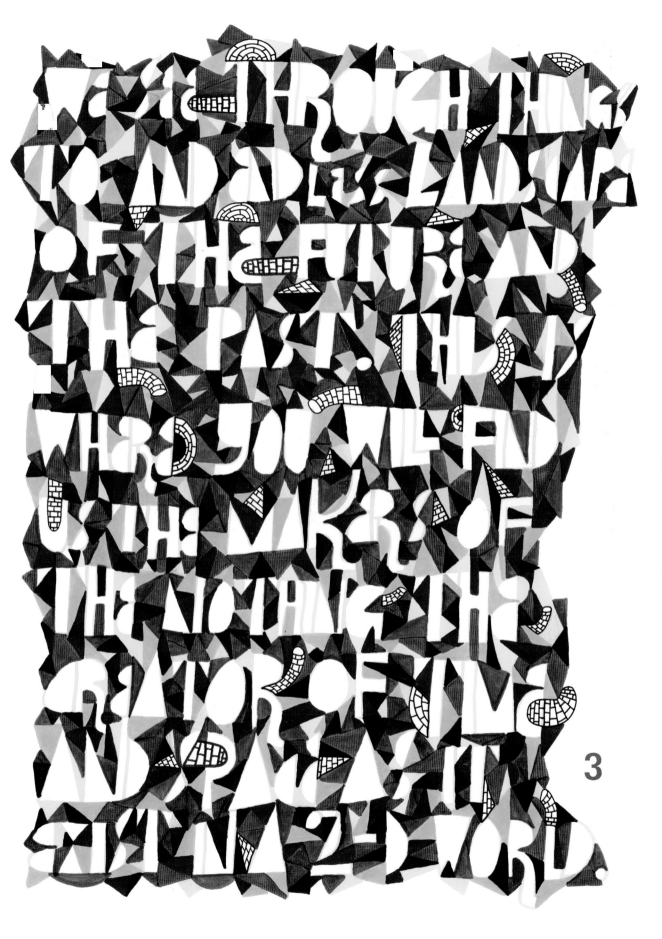

3

Kipi Ka Popo

Kipi Ka Popo is run by art director, designer, and illustrator Lydia Lapinski. Before setting up her studio in Sheffield, UK, Lydia worked at design agency Studio Output for a list of clients including the BBC, USC clothing brand, Coca-Cola, and UK television network Channel 4. Following this, Lydia went on to work at The Designers Republic for a list of clients including Coca-Cola, Littlest Pet Shop, and Arjowiggins. In 2008 Lydia left The Designers Republic to set up Kipi Ka Popo, which specializes in graphic design, branding, illustration, animation, web design, 3D design, textile design, plush toys, and set design.

1 This food-inspired illustration, titled Noodle Doodle, *was created using paper and Sharpie marker pens.*
2 This balloon-inspired logo design was created for the Kipi Ka Popo website.
3 This self-initiated illustration, titled Ahoy, *was created using paper and Sharpie marker pens, and then retouched in Photoshop. Lydia took her inspiration from the Michel Gondry film,* The Science of Sleep, *and the action-adventure video game* The Legend of Zelda.
4 Lydia likes to collect owl-related items. This illustration was inspired by a rumor that there was an owl living on her street.

1

2

3

4

Drawing and Painting_Showcase

Mysterious Al

Mysterious Al studied fine art at Falmouth College of Arts (now University College Falmouth), UK, and lives and works in London. He was an original member of the Finders Keepers Crew, who staged impromptu street art exhibitions in London, with the location only being revealed at the last minute by e-mail, and where free artwork was handed out. Mysterious Al has an impressive list of clients, including Carhartt, Volvo, Vans, and Eastpak. While his work has roots in the street art genre, it also manages to cross boundaries between illustration, graffiti, and fine art.

1–2 Painted using household emulsion and spray paint in Melbourne, Australia, and Spain.
3 Part of an installation painted with Matt Sewell (see pages 14–15) for the Greenhouse Gallery space in Guernsey, Channel Islands.

1

2

3

Susann Stefanizen

Susann Stefanizen is a graphic designer and illustrator based in Berlin, Germany. Susann studied at Hochschule Anhalt, Fachbereich Design Dessau (Department of Design) in Germany, during which time she gained experience working for the award-winning Fons Hickmann m23 studio in Berlin. Susann's work combines handmade and digital techniques. Her ambition is to open a small gallery in Berlin showcasing her own work alongside work by other upcoming designers and illustrators.

1–3 Drawings on paper with neon pink and blue gel ink pens. Susann takes her inspiration from daily encounters and old photographs.

1

2

3

Federico Martinez Aquino

Federico Martinez Aquino (aka El Feder) lives in Buenos Aires, Argentina, and works as a freelance graphic designer and stencil artist. His favorite method is stencil art mixed with handpainted and computer-generated imagery. His influences include music, movies, the streets, friends, Art Chantry, Saul Bass, Andy Warhol, horror movies, The Rolling Stones, punk rock, Jean-Michel Basquiat, Russ Meyer, B movies, and Bauhaus. Federico has been featured in numerous Argentinean magazines, and his work has been exhibited internationally.

1–2 These panels were painted for an exhibition at UADE Art Institute in Buenos Aires. The pieces consisted of handpainted and stenciled elements.

1

2

David Bradley

David Bradley studied fine art and sculpture at Sheffield Hallam University, UK. He has since worked as a creative practitioner within the fields of illustration and sculpture, and as a designer within the film industry. David's artworks are a result of drawing freehand using a graphics tablet and a combination of computer generated processes and intuitive physical movements. His ambitions include continuing to develop his visual language and to produce more multidisciplinary works, both individually and collaboratively.

1–3 These pieces were hand-drawn into Photoshop and Illustrator using a graphics tablet. David repeatedly draws playful organic shapes and adds, sculpts, and composes them together to visually represent the dichotomy between free will and determinism.

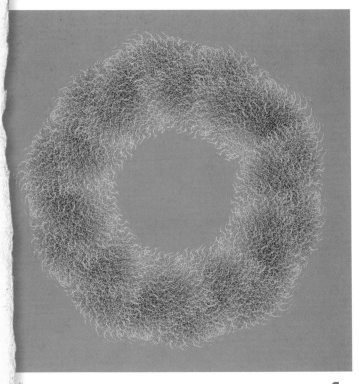

1

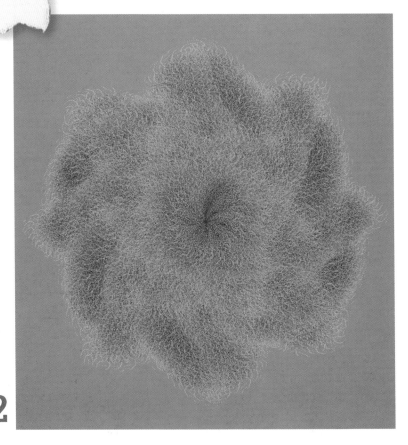

2

PEN AND INK:
Marion Lindsay

Pen and ink is ideal if you like the look of line drawings. However, many people are put off using dip pens by their first frustrating, often blobby, experiments. The only way you will be able to find the combination of ink, nib, and paper that best suits you is by trial and error. Dip pens are versatile to work with and give you the ability to make a great range of marks by varying the weight of the line, density, direction, and pattern. What I love about the mark from a dip pen is the way it tapers according to the amount of pressure applied, giving it a highly expressive quality. When you're starting out, it's a good idea to buy a few nib holders and a range of nibs so that you can easily compare their effects. When using pen and ink, it's also best to use paper with a smooth finish.

Materials
⇨ Pencil
⇨ Paper
⇨ Ink pen
⇨ Drawing nibs
⇨ White ink
⇨ Paintbrush

Artist bio
⇨ Marion Lindsay is a freelance illustrator and artist who works primarily on children's picture books. She lives in Cambridge, UK.

01 Begin by sketching your picture in pencil, and then outline the main characters using an ink pen. The characters are what the picture is all about; if you get them wrong at this stage, it's quick enough to start again. Ink is not easy to change or remove, so you are always committing yourself to the marks you make. It is therefore important to get the foundation of your picture right. As you move along and work on other elements there is some room for error. I think that at this stage it's good to know you can throw the picture away if it doesn't look right—it takes the pressure off and makes it easier to create an image that retains the spontaneity of the idea behind it.

02 Next I have created trees in the foreground using widely spaced, short parallel lines. I wanted to convey the texture of the bark on the tree without being too precise, and to also give the trees an overall medium tone that would sit somewhere between the light of the foreground and the dark of the sky. I added a squirrel too, for no other reason than because they're nice!

03 I then added a second row of trees using the same marks, but drawn closer together, in order to create a denser effect. My aim was to make these trees feel further away and also to distinguish them from the foreground trees. My little squirrel's legs have somewhat disappeared into the tree behind, but I will fix this later on.

04 I used a cross-hatching technique made up of lines that vary in direction for the sky. The idea was to create a dark area, but leave lots of little white marks that weren't too uniform and resembled snow. Cross-hatching is a great way to build up tone; it is extremely controllable in the sense that you can use it to achieve a whole range of tones, and can also be given a uniform or divergent look depending on the requirements of the picture.

05 My image is beginning to come together. I have added in some further details that I think help make the image feel more solid and rounded. I like to put patterns in my pictures as I think they can be a way to help give form without being too obvious—pen and ink is great for adding in this kind of detail because you can add thin lines easily.

06 Now it's time to add the finishing touches. This is where I get to cheat and use white ink! I used a brush and splodged on as much snow as I thought I could get away with. I also added white lines to the squirrel's legs so they were more distinct from the tree behind. It's fine to touch up parts of a black and white drawing with white ink so long as the picture is for publication. If it's destined to be framed then you need to get it right the first time round, as white ink will be obvious on the paper. (See final image opposite.)

FELT-TIP PENS:
Emily Robertson

Felt-tip pens are a great medium to draw with, especially as there are a large choice of nib weights and colors to choose from. Because of this they are also versatile—they're good for fine line work as well as blocks of instant color. This workthrough demonstrates how to draw a robin. Birds make ideal drawing subjects because they're so cute and colorful. I am quite nerdy about my pens; my favorites are the STABILO Pen 68 variety. They are a delight to use and are ideal for strong lines and large areas. Before you start drawing, make sure you have a range of pens handy, and always use pens with a fine tip in areas of detail.

erithacus rubecula

the robin has ... a thin, rather sad b
sweet warbling song, consisting of
phrases

Materials
➪ Lead pencil
➪ Paper or card
➪ Artist felt-tip pens with various tips
➪ Eraser

Artist bio
➪ Emily Robertson is a UK-based freelance illustrator and is one of the founders of the artist's group Plats.

01 I'm not sure what comes first when I decide to do a drawing—the idea, or knowing what medium I'm going to use. With felt-tip pens you can make lovely textures and layers, so it's for this reason that I like drawing birds. Here I started with a pencil sketch of an outline of the bird and the blocks that I wanted to fill in with different colors and patterns.

02 I next thought about the quality of the felt-tip pens I was using, chose my colors, and warmed up my hand. If you haven't drawn for a while it's a good idea to get your hand used to making quick, smooth lines. I started filling in the blocks using small rows of lines. While doing this I altered the tones of color—here I mixed two shades of red in order to suggest feathers.

03 Filling in the bird's breast area has turned it into a more rounded object and added shape, which is always the most exciting part for me. It provides an understanding of how the drawing is going to work, and whether or not it will be a success.

04 Next I sketched some more outlines and erased the lines I wasn't happy with or didn't need anymore. It is usually at this time that I decide to take a break, have a cup of tea, and think about what I am going to do next. Drawing is a terribly tiring business!

05 I thought about the overall drawing and how to make it interesting to look at, and started coloring in the wing patterns. I also rubbed out more of the pencil lines I didn't need.

06 Here I changed the felt-tip color and filled in the rest of the pattern on the wing and tail areas, mixing the strokes of the pens and the density of the lines. This added more interest to the drawing rather than a boring block of color. I like to use lead pencil in my illustrations; here I used it for the eye and legs, and the contrast between the two mediums is visually pleasing.

07 At this point I like to add detail with a darker felt-tip shade, adding shapes and defining features to make the drawing come alive. I also reworked areas I wasn't happy with, such as correcting the bird's eye and finishing off the beak.

08 I added the final details on the robin with a gray felt-tip pen, and used soft pen strokes to suggest feathers. I then cleaned up any stray lines and unnecessary pencil marks, and checked the drawing as a whole. (See final image opposite.)

SPRAY-PAINTED MURAL: Matt Sewell

This spray-painted mural is based on one of my watercolor paintings. I wanted to experiment with new ways of developing this character, and seeing as how spray paint is such an experimental and exciting medium, it seemed ideal. It's also great to take your work out of the studio and paint in the fresh air whenever possible.

Materials
⇨ Chalk
⇨ White emulsion
⇨ Spray paint (I used dark purple, light purple, sky blue, and white)

Tools
⇨ Mini paint roller
⇨ Paint tray

01 I began by finding a spot for my mural. This wall already had graffiti on it surrounded by a certain element of urban decay, so was ideal. The first thing I did was chalk up some guidelines ready to paint the foundation layer. It's a good idea to do this before you start spraying as it allows you to step back and see if the proportions of the image will work within the context of the wall.

02 Next I painted the wall with an emulsion undercoat using a mini paint roller. This seals the wall and provides a good spraying surface by stopping the porous concrete from soaking up too much spray paint. The white background will also give the colors more vibrancy later on.

03 I outlined the basic face and hair shapes in dark purple spray paint with quick, controlled strokes, and then filled them in. This formed a nice, simple shape in preparation for the more detailed aspects of the design.

04 To gain more control (this is especially useful when using cheaper cans of spray paint), put a small amount of paper between the nozzle and the can. This eases the pressure and slows the paint down. This trick can only be used with female nozzles.

05 Pressing down on the nozzle at half pressure allowed me to gain just the right amount of control needed to create the nebula, beams, and cosmic mist. I did this by making straight, quick lines using my whole arm and spraying slowly and at a distance to achieve a more misty effect.

06 Here I wanted to use the paint without spraying. Thankfully, cans have a ready-made well at the bottom, so I sprayed a bit of white paint into the well to work from.

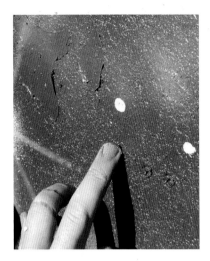

07 To make the stars I dipped my finger into the paint and dabbed it onto the wall, which produced a nice, hard-edged contrast to the spray effect. There are many different ways of using spray paint—don't just stick to the obvious!

08 Here I spray painted light blue over the dark blue area in order to add depth to the misty stars. There is now a nice balance between flatness of color and a more layered, shaded use of paint.

09 Now comes one of the most crucial parts of the piece: adding detail to the faces. I don't like to cut lines back and sharpen the image too much as I feel this can make it lose character. If I mess up this step I generally paint over it and start again. The eyes needed to be fluid, and to achieve this I quickly sprayed them in one go. This face is very in keeping with my style so I have lots of practice drawing like this. However, if you don't feel confident I would recommend practicing on another bit of wall or surface first—it will be worth it in the end!

Artist bio
⇨ Matt Sewell is a UK-based graphic artist. More of his work can be seen on pages 14–15.
All photos by Ikool.

10 After coloring the eyes using just a few short sprays, I then painted the outlines using long, fluid strokes in three different colors (white, light purple, and dark purple). It's very important to me to limit my colors to three or four—too many colors can complicate an image and make it lose its strong graphic simplicity.

11 Finally, the mural is finished. All I have left to do now is stand back and admire my handiwork!

HAND-DRAWN TYPE:
Jesse Hora Dot Com

I am a self-confessed type nerd. There are so many creative ways to treat type, and typography doesn't have to stop at downloading fonts from the internet— it really can be the ultimate form of expression and creativity. I like to draw animals, figures, and patterns within my type. I have a love of the unexpected and try to push the boundaries within my typography. In this tutorial I will show you how to create intricate and complex hand-drawn typography from start to finish, and I hope that it inspires you to create your own unique type.

Materials
⇨ Pencil
⇨ Drawing pen
⇨ Paper
⇨ Tracing paper

Hardware
⇨ Scanner
⇨ Printer

Software
⇨ Illustrator

 Thinking about

01 Before I began, I thought about the word I wanted to draw. I like to play with words visually, and since this tutorial was about hand-drawn type, the word "type" was ideal. As a starting point I printed out the word in a Modern Sans Serif font and traced over it in pencil.

02 Take time to compose your drawing. Think of it as the framework of a house—if the foundation isn't solid then the house is going to crumble. Here I sketched over the type with ornaments and swirls. Experiment for yourself and erase and draw again if need be—it's important to get this stage just right.

03 Next I scanned my sketch and adjusted it in Illustrator, fixing any awkward areas. Once complete, I printed out a hairline version and drew directly onto the page. This helped me stay on track and keep an eye on the entire composition.

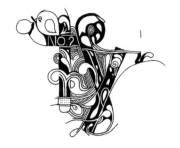

04 This is where the fun begins, and diving right in with ink is the only way to go. I started by drawing little animal-like shapes and connecting everything with complex line patterns using a drawing pen (I use a Pilot DR drawing pen with a variety of nib weights). For example, on the letter "T" you can see the start of an upside-down turtle, which also looks like the eraser on the end of a pencil.

05 This is when it's time to start experimenting—draw anything and everything. I like to pack as much line work into the letterforms as possible in order to achieve a complex look. You will need to establish how you are going to handle the letterforms so that it will be constant throughout the drawing. I like to vary the letterforms quite a bit by adding shapes and lines to break things up, while still keeping the readability in mind.

06 At this point I like to zone out and crank up the music, grab a beverage, and go to town. I guess this is where the psychedelic elements of my work are introduced because I don't consciously think about what I'm drawing; I just draw. Here I have started to finish things off and add intricate details. For example, I have drawn a little bird with a speech bubble into the negative space of the "T." Isn't he cute?

07 Once finished I scanned my drawing. Sometimes I like to fill the entire composition on all sides with doodles and line work, but for this piece I decided I liked the overall shape as it was.

08 Finally, I opened my scanned drawing in Illustrator and made it into a vector file, which allowed me to scale the image as large as possible and achieve a sharp, clean, black-and-white graphic style. I used the Live Trace function in Illustrator to trace the image and clean up the drawing. Above is the final, clean drawing.

Artist bio
⇨ Jesse Hora Dot Com is a Chicago-based freelance graphic artist. You can see more of his work on pages 80–81.

PRINTING

This chapter showcases the work of artists and designers who use a variety of traditional and contemporary printmaking techniques and processes.

Because printmaking has the ability to create a multitude of visual qualities, it is an area that proves to be irresistible to designers, illustrators, and artists. This popularity is supported by a multitude of international university degrees and masters courses that either specialize in or incorporate printmaking within the course structure. The creative practitioners featured in this chapter all have a unique approach to printmaking, both in terms of technique and application, be it woodblock, linoprinting, screenprinting, or etching. For example, the alphabet featured in graphic designer Susan Carey's unique print (see pages 76–77) was created by contorting and shaping paper clips. The final result was achieved through a process of photocopying and screenprinting, and is a unique example of handmade type that has stayed true to its lo-fi beginnings.

Typographer Will Hill uses the letterpress printing method and breaks its associated traditions as one of the oldest forms of printing by employing letters as compositional, rather than informational, visual devices. His prints therefore work on an abstract level, simultaneously examining the boundaries between function and form (see pages 54–55). Graphic designer Jacqueline Ford also uses letterpress as the primary method for her work. She creates meticulous and complex three-color images out of tiny letterpress blocks. Here we also see letterpress taken out of its traditional context, and instead used to create new and interesting images (see pages 72–73).

1

2

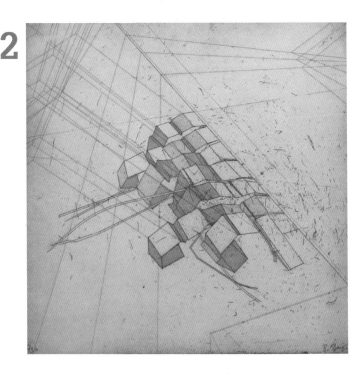

1 By Modern Dog, see pages 52–53.
2 By Bronwen Sleigh, see pages 74–75.
3 By Sarah King, see pages 66–67.
2 By Gemma Anderson, see pages 62–63.

Screenprinting is a popular medium used by artists, crafters, designers, and illustrators alike. Luisa Uribe is one artist showcased in this chapter who plays upon the inherently flat nature of two-color screenprinting by layering and contrasting images. The results are visually intriguing prints that constantly shift focus and play with pictorial space and form (see pages 56–57).

Linocutting is another printing technique showcased in this chapter. A wide audience first saw Stanley Donwood's linocuts when they were used on the artwork for the Thom Yorke album, *The Eraser*. Donwood uses the ancient technique of woodcutting, but applies it to linoleum to create a modern, apocalyptic view of London sinking and burning under the weight of the consequences of Western capitalism (see pages 64–65).

Finally, etching is another printmaking process that can either be simple or complex depending on the desired result. Artist Gemma Anderson uses this age-old method to create fine, delicate etchings; her work explores the anatomical relationship between plants, animals, objects, and humans (see pages 62–63). In contrast, Bronwen Sleigh's etchings explore an industrial theme. Her prints are made up of a complex series of lines that depict an often bleak, but strangely compelling, post-industrialized landscape (see pages 74–75).

Printing is one of the more complex and involved methods showcased in this book; however, not all printing requires a fully equipped studio. Linocutting, for example, can be achieved with basic materials, as Charlie and Sarah Adams demonstrate on pages 90–91. Likewise, Gluekit take us through the screenprinting process using basic equipment that can easily be set up at home (see pages 84–86). For more ambitious printers, many towns and cities have printing studios that run courses or open-access sessions, and it's well worth the effort seeking them out. Happy printing!

4

Modern Dog

Founded in Seattle in 1987, Modern Dog Design Co. is an internationally acclaimed design agency that specializes in creating imaginative, bold, and playful designs in interactive and print medias. Current and past clients include the Seattle Aquarium, Disney, Swatch, K2 Snowboarding, HarperCollins, Nordstrom, Blue Q, and *The New York Times*. They have two office dogs named Winnifred and Conran, and in 2008 Chronicle Books released *Modern Dog: 20 Years of Poster Art (Not Canine-Related)*, a collection of their poster designs.

1 This gig poster was created for the band The Sea and Cake. Originally a collage, this final poster was screenprinted in two colors.

2 The wolf in this poster was carved out of a piece of plywood and the type was created by hand with pen and ink and tidied up in Illustrator. The final poster shown here is a three-color screenprint.

3 This poster was created for an AIGA Raleigh lecture, titled Modern Dog Unleashed. *The illustration and lettering were created by hand using stencils and Sumi ink and were then scanned. The final poster was screenprinted in black ink, and four additional colors (red, yellow, purple, and green) were applied by hand.*

1

2

Will Hill

Will Hill studied at Winchester School of Art and Cambridge School of Art in the UK, and practiced as a freelance designer, illustrator, design consultant, and typographer from 1977 to 1993. During this time he worked for publications such as *Time Out*, *New Scientist*, *New Statesman*, *New Society*, *Radio Times*, *The Observer*, and *The Sunday Telegraph*. Will has a fascination for lettering and type specimens, which he admits borders upon the obsessive. He is a graphic design lecturer at the Cambridge School of Art, UK, and exhibits his letterpress typographic work nationally and internationally.

1–4 In this self-initiated project a series of fragments from early rural blues lyrics were set in a variety of wooden letterpress type and proofed in black on a flatbed proofing press. Multiple proofs were made, allowing Will to explore the effects of varying degrees of under-inking. The proofs were then scanned and assembled in Photoshop, and color and scale were manipulated digitally. The final compositions shown here were printed from a large-format digital printer.

1

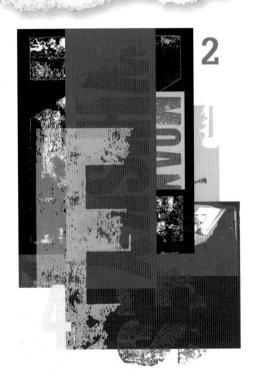

2

3

Luisa Uribe

Originally from Bogotá, Colombia, Luisa studied art and design at the Loughborough University School of Art and Design in the UK. Since returning to Bogotá she has worked as a freelance illustrator for a number of international clients from her home studio. Luisa has exhibited her work widely alongside the likes of Jon Burgerman (see pages 24–25) and Si Scott. She takes her main inspiration from books, movies, people, and cats.

1 *This T-shirt design was created by scanning a pencil drawing and adding color layers in Photoshop. The image was then transferred to a screen and printed by hand.*
2 *This two-color poster, created for the* Blisters On My Fingers *exhibition at Print Club London in 2008, was drawn directly into Photoshop on separate layers. It was then transferred to screens and printed by hand.*

1

Jenny Wilkinson

Jenny Wilkinson studied at Chelsea College of Art & Design and Brighton University in the UK. She is an independent designer and lecturer and set up her own design studio in 2003. Her portfolio of work includes wallpaper and textile designs, as well as surface design using wood, metal, ceramics, and plastics. Jenny is best known for her Wallpaper-By-Numbers interactive wallpaper collection, a range of wallpapers inspired by the classic paint-by-numbers craze, which was acquired by the Victoria and Albert Museum in London for their permanent collection.

The images shown here are part of Jenny's Wallpaper-By-Numbers collection. They are designed to be painted in small sections or left as simple outlines.

1–2 Venus Flutterby was inspired by Venus flytraps. The original hand-drawn images were scanned, and the repeat pattern was then created digitally.

3 Gerbera was created as a simple floral pattern, and was inspired by traditional wallpaper designs.

4 Pineapple was inspired by 1950s retro prints. It was created by scanning and digitally manipulating a photograph, before it was turned into a repeat pattern.

1

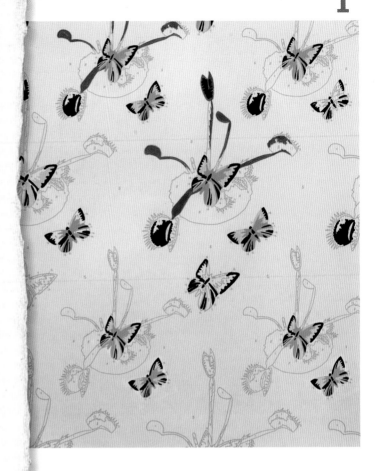

3

2

Harmen Liemburg

Harmen Liemburg studied at the Gerrit Rietveld Academie in the Netherlands and now works as a freelance designer, illustrator, and design journalist from his home studio in Amsterdam. He has been screenprinting his illustrations for a number of years, which he also exhibits and sells. His ambitions for the future include creating more spontaneous work, and he also plans to work on projects connected to architecture and textiles.

1 *Based on contemporary Japanese candy packaging, this silkscreened invitation was created for an installation at the SieboldHuis in Leiden, Netherlands.*
2 *This print, To Oceans of Joy, was created in collaboration with graphic designer Ed Fella. It celebrates their mutual love for the American vernacular. It was silkscreened in a limited edition of 50.*
3 *This limited-edition silkscreened souvenir poster was created for an installation at the 2005 Chaumont Poster Festival in France.*

1

2

Gemma Anderson

Gemma Anderson is a self-employed artist. She studied fine art at Falmouth College of Art and printmaking at the Royal College of Art in the UK. She has since undertaken artist residencies in France, Ireland, Italy, and Japan, and has exhibited internationally. Gemma's main medium is etching, although she also works in drawing, collage, and watercolor. Her work is inspired by early scientific theories and observations, phrenology, physiognomy, and theories regarding the resemblance between humans and animals.

1–3 The prints shown here (1, Gareth; 2, Susan; and 3, Alice) are part of Gemma's "People I Know" series. Each piece is a hand-colored etching measuring 31.5 × 40in/80 × 100cm, and limited to an edition of ten prints.

3

Stanley Donwood

Stanley Donwood is largely known for his close association with the British band Radiohead, for whom he has created various album and poster artworks. He lives and works as a freelance artist in Plymouth, UK, where he has a printing studio. He exhibits widely, and also writes and publishes his own books and stories online and in print.

1–4 Shown here are sections from Fleet Street Apocalypse, a 38 × 25in/96.5 × 63.5cm linoprint. The print shows Fleet Street in London up in flames, with a few survivors attempting to escape a flood sweeping along the street. The print was made on a Hopkinson & Cope printing press from 1844 using acid-free archival quality Somerset White 300gsm satin paper and Cranfield letterpress black ink. The print was also used on the artwork for the Thom Yorke album The Eraser.

1

2

3

4

Sarah King

After graduating from the University of
Brighton, UK, Sarah King had the opportunity
to spend three months as an intern in New
York with Mike Perry (see pages 28–29). This
proved to be an invaluable insight into the
creative industry. She then moved to London
and now works from her home studio as
a freelance illustrator. Her ambitions are
to continue drawing, printing, traveling, and
meeting new creative and inspirational people.

1 Seven Foot With A Woden Leg *was made for
an exhibition based around the theme of "self."
Sarah made a rough sketch in pencil, edited it
in Photoshop, and then turned it into a screenprint.
The text was taken from a book Sarah's father wrote.*
2 *This screenprinted poster was made as a proposal
for the Deutsche Börse Photography Prize.*

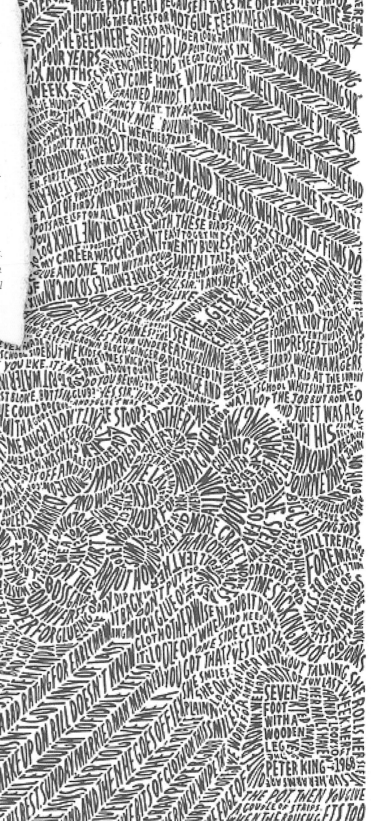

1

DISCOVER THE BEST OF INTERNATIONAL PHOTOGRAPHY
9TH FEBRUARY - 4TH APRIL
DEUTSCHE BORSE PHOTOGRAPHY PRIZE 2007
PHILIPPE CHANCEL
ANDERS PETERSON
FIONA TAN
WALID RAAD/ THE ATLAS GROUP
AT THE PHOTOGRAPHER'S GALLERY
5 AND 8 GREAT NEWPORT STREET
LONDON WC2H 7HY
ADMISSION FREE
NEAREST TUBE, LEICESTER SQUARE.
GALLERIES AND BOOKSHOP OPEN MON TO SAT,
11:00 - 18:00. THUR 11:00 - 20:00, SUN 12:00 - 19:00

2

Mack Manning

Mack Manning studied at Maidstone College of Art (now the University for the Creative Arts at Maidstone) and the Royal College of Art in London. Mack is based in the UK and works as an academic consultant and a senior lecturer at Manchester Metropolitan University. His design clients include Friends of the Earth, Penguin Books, the BBC, and British newspapers *The Observer*, *The Sunday Times*, and *The Independent*. Mack has also worked for The Body Shop International on special design projects for the United Nations. Mack takes inspiration from natural and rural history, landscape, and memory.

1 Titled Jump, *this is a collaged carbon monoprint.*
2 One with Wishes, *a monoprint purchased by the Whitworth Art Gallery in Manchester, UK, for their permanent collection.*
3 *Print created as cover art for a collection of short stories by M. R. James.*

1

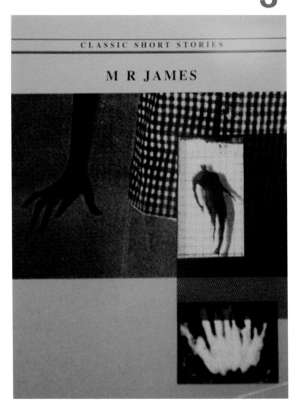

3

2

Kirk Whayman

Kirk Whayman studied graphic design at Norwich University College of the Arts in the UK. He is undertaking a masters in printmaking at Cambridge School of Art and also works as a designer. His favorite mediums to work with are illustration and screenprinting, and his work is based around his own personal history, often using old family photographs as a starting point and then adding collaged elements to them. Kirk's goal is to continue exhibiting and to set up his own design agency.

1–2 Self-initiated works printed onto photographic paper. Kirk takes his inspiration from old family photo albums.

1

2

Chrissie Abbott

Chrissie Abbott lives and works in London. She studied at The London College of Communication and worked at Zip Design agency before becoming a freelance illustrator and graphic designer for clients including *NYLON* magazine, *The Guardian*, *Wired*, *The New York Times*, and *Dazed & Confused* magazine. She has also been featured in *PAGE*, *Sonic* magazine, and the Taschen book, *Illustration Now!*. Her most enjoyable work to date has been creating artwork for UK musician Little Boots, which included developing merchandise and artwork for print and web.

1 Jellyfish, a self-initiated drawing that was then turned into a screenprint.
2 Inspired by The Beatles song "Blackbird," Chrissie combined collaged elements, hand-drawn patterns, and screenprinting methods to create this wedding invite.
3 Images of crystals were used to create this type and were then screenprinted using a gradient.
4 This is a T-shirt design for 2K By Gingham. Chrissie drew the pattern work, created the final image in Photoshop, and then created a screenprint.

1

2 3

MORE
THAN
REAL

4

Jacqueline Ford

Jacqueline Ford studied graphic design and illustration at the London College of Communication. Her favorite mediums to work with include lead, ink, and a galley press. She exhibited work in *The Changing Face of Letterpress* exhibition at the London College of Communication in 2009, where her letterpress tiger head (opposite) was featured on the promotional materials.

1–2 Prints composed and printed from various letterpress ornaments, created for The Changing Face of Letterpress.

2

Bronwen Sleigh

After graduating from the Glasgow School of Art in Scotland, Bronwen Sleigh studied printmaking at the Royal College of Art in London. Bronwen predominantly works within etching, and is inspired by modern architecture and industrial landscapes. She completed an artist in residency at the Highland Print Studio in Inverness, Scotland, and has since exhibited widely.

Bronwen's prints are made using Somerset paper, etching ink, and steel plates, which she prepares using hardground wax and nitric acid. She is heavily influenced by industrial architectural spaces.

1–2 These pieces (Brentwood and 48th Avenue S E) *were produced using etching and screenprinting methods, and were made during Bronwen's residency in Calgary, Canada. They were influenced by the architecture and spaces she found within the city.*

3 & 5 These etchings are based on Nigg, a disused oil yard in Scotland. Nigg was one of the first places that sparked Bronwen's interest in industrial architecture.

4 Turbine II *is an etching that was produced for Bronwen's first solo show at the Glasgow Print Studio, Scotland, in 2005.*

1

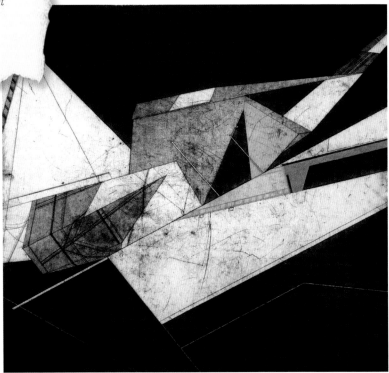

2

3

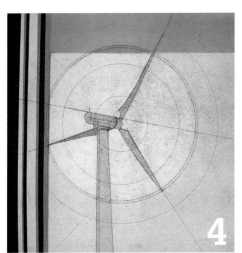

4

5

Susan Carey

After graduating from Newcastle College in the UK, Susan Carey began her creative career designing newspapers and magazines, eventually becoming art editor at *Empire* magazine. She now works as a freelance graphic designer for various consumer magazines and design clients mainly within the music, radio, and comedy sectors. Susan is also a passionate photographer and experimental typographer.

1 This alphabet was created during an experimental typography course Susan attended at the London College of Communication, UK. Susan photocopied paper clips, enlarged them, and then cut and pasted them into an alphabet form.

1

Niessen & de Vries

Niessen & de Vries is an Amsterdam-based studio run by Richard Niessen and Esther de Vries. Niessen & de Vries regularly work for clients in the creative and cultural sectors, and also initiate exhibitions, books, lectures, and workshops.

1 This screenprinted poster was made for the opening of the Kong design store in Mexico City, Mexico. Richard took inspiration from King Kong and the computer games Pong *and* Donkey Kong *to create a cityscape built out of the letters K, O, N, and G.*

2 This screenprinted poster was made when Niessen & de Vries moved studios. It was created using Richard's hand-drawn Scram C Baby font.

3 This screenprinted poster was created for a lecture Niessen & de Vries gave at the Hochschule für Künsten Bremen (University of the Arts), Germany. The words have been overlaid in oppose directions, and the poster is designed to also be hung upside down.

1

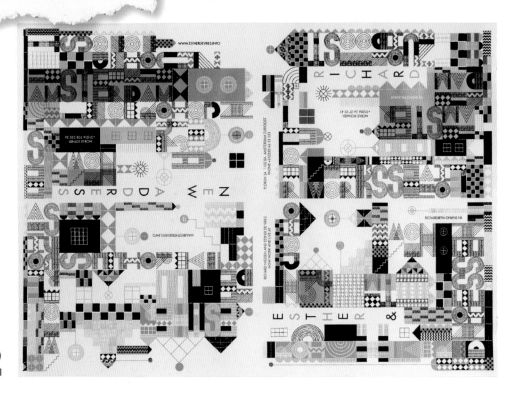

2

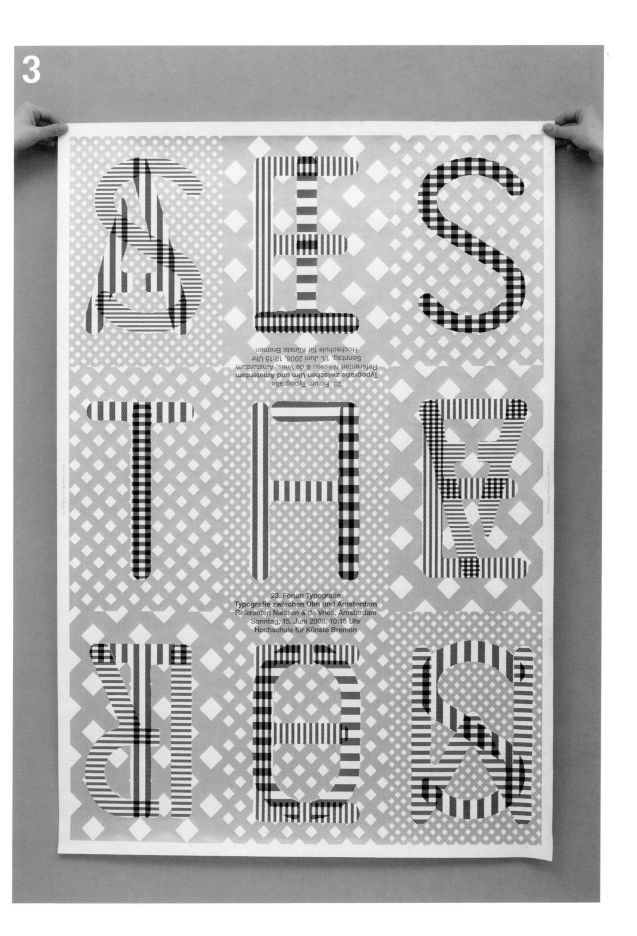

Jesse Hora Dot Com

Jesse's love of drawing began as a child, and this led him to a degree in graphic design at Grand Valley State University, USA. Jesse lives in Chicago and works from his home studio. He has built up an impressive list of clients, including adidas Originals, Warner Bros. + Reprise Records, *BPM Magazine*, Mountain Dew, OfficeMax, Bubblicious, *Chicago* magazine, Sims Snowboards, *Computer Arts Magazine*, and Miller Brewing Company. His dreams include opening a creative firm (and moving to a deserted island with his girlfriend and dog). Jesse enjoys working with the classic medium of pen and pencil on paper, and his inspiration comes from handpainted signs, wide receivers, patterns, food, old medical illustrations, and hair!

1–2 Created as part of the "Somethin' Somethin'"
series, these two pieces were drawn, scanned,
and retouched in Photoshop before being Gocco
printed with multiple inks on textured paper stock.
3 Whenitrainsitpours *is a self-initiated intricate*
typographic silkscreen poster, originally created
using pen and paper.

1

pick up your
pencils people!

lead
aint
dead

2

Amy and Joe
are getting
married!

1

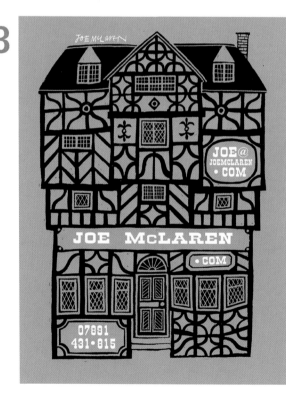

JOHN
BETJEMAN

ff

Poems selected by
HUGO
WILLIAMS

2

3

Joe McLaren

Joe McLaren began his professional illustration
career after graduating from the University of
Brighton, UK, in 2003. He has done work for
The Times, *Wired*, and *Computer Arts*. He
has also illustrated a number of book covers
for publishing companies including White's
Books, John Murray, Faber & Faber, and
Portobello Books.

1 This Gocco print was created as a wedding invitation.
*2 Joe used a scraperboard method to create this book
cover. The effect replicates the impression and clean
contrast of woodcutting.*
*3 This self-promotional postcard was also created
using a scraperboard method.*
*4 This limited-edition letterpress print of a magic castle
was created for Wilkintie, a fine art letterpress store.*

4

SCREENPRINTED POSTER: Gluekit

Making a screenprint is a great way to get your hands dirty and create something tactile and one-of-a-kind. For us, the act of printing also provides an opportunity to render graphics and type in an approachable and unique way. One of the things we love about screenprinting is the possibility of imperfection and the kind of spontaneity that it invites. Having the proper space and tools is important, but we also enjoy the challenge of being creative and clever enough to make do with what we have. If you're determined and persistent you too can make prints that translate your personal vision.

Tools
- Table or other flat surface
- Jiffy clamps
- Emulsion scoop
- Squeegee
- Screen
- Glass pane
- Clamp lamp
- 500W lightbulb

Materials
- Emulsion
- Black paper or fabric
- Non-porous tape
- Acrylic water-based screenprinting ink
- Paper or card

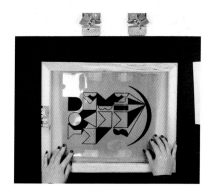

01 Begin by creating your artwork digitally or by hand, and then scan and edit it on computer. Adjust the levels to make sure the image is nice and sharp and that it has lots of contrast. Be careful not to make your lines too thin, especially if you are just starting out. Figure out what size screen you will be using and adjust the dimensions of your artwork appropriately, and then print out your image.

02 Prepare your workstation. You'll need a large, smooth tabletop with plenty of space to spread out. We went to our local hardware store and purchased a sheet of melamine to use as our portable screenprinting station, which can be laid on top of a waist-high worktable. Screw a pair of jiffy clamps directly onto your table or board to hold your screen in place.

03 Prepare the emulsion by following the instructions on the pot (we use Speedball Diazo Photo Emulsion). You'll be combining chemicals, shaking them up, and adding them to different containers, so it's important to read the instructions. Preparing emulsion is kind of like dyeing your hair at home, except you should prepare it in low light. Pour the emulsion mixture onto one side of the screen and spread it evenly and smoothly with an emulsion scoop, squeegee, or a sturdy piece of cardboard. Coat both sides of the screen. When you're done, place the screen in a dark place for 1–2 hours.

04 Prepare the screen for exposure. This step should occur in your makeshift darkroom. After the emulsion has dried completely, place a large piece of black paper on your table followed by your screen (printing side down), then your artwork (right side up), and top the stack off with a pane of glass large enough to cover your artwork. If you don't have glass, try dismantling a picture frame; if you don't have black paper you can use fabric—the idea is to back the frame with something that won't reflect light back onto your screen during exposure.

05 Set up a clamp lamp with a 500W bulb. Place it directly over your screen, about 1½ ft (45cm) away, turn it on, and let it focus on your artwork for 20 minutes. Once the time is up, rinse your screen immediately under running water. Your design should appear like magic. The areas that were black on your transparency should look like the clean screen before you applied the emulsion, while emulsion will have filled the areas that were clear in your artwork. Wash the screen thoroughly, but be careful to avoid over-rinsing—you want the emulsion to stay in the areas it's supposed to!

06 When your screen is dry, tape the edges with several layers of non-porous tape, which will restrict the areas where ink can be applied to the clear elements of your design. Lay down several layers of tape to make sure no ink will seep through.

07 Fix your screen in place with the clamps and make sure your ink, squeegee, and printing paper are nearby.

08 Using a spatula, apply acrylic water-based screenprinting ink (for paper, not fabric) along the top of your screen. Don't be afraid to glop the ink on. We often use an extra jar of ink to prop up our screen in order to make the ink application easier.

09 Lift up your inked screen and slide some nice thick paper underneath (we use Bristol Board). There are many ways you can help yourself align the position of the paper in relation to the screen. Making crop marks with removable artist tape works well and helps to make consistently positioned prints.

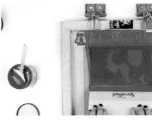

12 Carefully lift your screen and place your print on a rack (or somewhere safe) and allow it to dry. If you are doing more than one print, try to work in a fairly quick manner, adding new ink when necessary. Once finished, wash the ink off your screen and allow it to dry.

10 In order to avoid lines in your final print, make sure you have a squeegee that's big enough to cover the whole width of your design. Position it at the top of your screen so that a well of ink is between the squeegee and your art.

11 Start at the top of the screen and pull your squeegee firmly and steadily toward you, drawing ink over the whole of your design.

Artist bio
⇨ Gluekit are a US-based design agency that specializes in illustration, graphic design, and lettering. More of their work can be found on pages 118–119.

ETCHING:
Laura Jacometti

My work is inspired by the designs and decorative images used on Dutch delftware pottery. These white ornaments often feature blue flower arrangements and other decorative images. I have chosen etching for this project because of its sharp, fine lines, and by using black ink, the images appear removed from their traditional context. The aim of this piece is to show a traditional decorative image in a new and different light.

Materials
⇨ Pen
⇨ Paper
⇨ Denatured alcohol
   (methylated spirits)
⇨ Cloth
⇨ Etching plate
⇨ Whiting powder
⇨ Ammonia
⇨ Hardground wax
⇨ Stop-out varnish
⇨ Acid bath
⇨ Metal file
⇨ Black etching ink
⇨ Printmaking paper

Tools
⇨ Roller
⇨ Paintbrush
⇨ Drypoint needle
⇨ Scrim
⇨ Magnifying glass

01 I started by drawing an image that I wanted to base my etching on.

02 Clean the etching plate with the denatured alcohol and a clean, dry cloth.

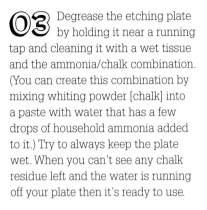

03 Degrease the etching plate by holding it near a running tap and cleaning it with a wet tissue and the ammonia/chalk combination. (You can create this combination by mixing whiting powder [chalk] into a paste with water that has a few drops of household ammonia added to it.) Try to always keep the plate wet. When you can't see any chalk residue left and the water is running off your plate then it's ready to use.

04 After the etching plate is dry, place it on a hotplate. You should be able to find a hotplate in a good printing studio. Once the plate is warm, place a small amount of hardground wax onto it and coat the wax over the plate's surface with a roller. The purpose of the wax is to create a seal on the metal that will resist the acid. Once you draw into the plate it will remove the wax and create a line ready to etch when the plate is placed in acid.

05 Paint the back of your plate with stop-out varnish and let it dry. This ensures that the back of the plate doesn't come into contact with the acid and dissolve the metal when you place it into the acid. Therefore, only the lines drawn into the metal will be in contact with the acid and will show.

06 Place your drawing (or a photocopy or trace) onto the prepared plate and draw over it with a pen (or something similar), which will make a slight imprint into the wax. You can secure the drawing with masking tape onto the surface if you wish. Remove the drawing once you've finished—you should see the image lightly engraved onto the plate.

07 At this point you can scratch the image further into the wax with a drypoint needle or sharp tool, making sure the wax is taken away and the plate surface is visible in the drawn areas. This is where the acid will bite away at the metal, creating an indentation on the plate's surface that will hold the ink when printing.

08 Place the etching plate into the acid bath. The longer you leave the plate in the acid the darker the lines will be. This is because the lines get deeper the more the acid erodes the metal, and they will therefore hold more ink when printing. Check whether the acid has bitten the lines enough with a magnifying glass.

09 Run the plate under water and then clean the wax off with a cloth and the denatured alcohol. File the edges of the plate with a metal file so that they won't cut through the blankets of the press or the paper.

10 Rub the etching ink onto your plate with a piece of cardboard or a roller. The cardboard helps to push the ink into the grooves in a scraping motion.

11 Wipe your plate clean with a scrim, making sure the ink has seeped into the lines but is minimal on the surface, unless you want a very dark image. The plate is now ready to press.

12 Place a slightly damp piece of paper onto the etching plate and print by rolling the plate and paper together through an etching press (any good printing studio should have this facility).

Artist bio

↪ After completing a textiles and art history degree in Amsterdam, Laura moved to the UK to study footwear and accessories design at Cordwainers College (now Cordwainers at The London College of Fashion) in London. Laura worked as a footwear designer for ten years for various companies before becoming a freelance designer. She is now undertaking an MA in printmaking at the Cambridge School of Art in the UK.

BLOCK PRINTING:
Charlie & Sarah Adams

Our printmaking career began when we were preparing for our wedding. After creating numerous handmade invitations and notecards, we decided to turn our hobby into a small business. Printmaking is our favorite design method. We use a variety of materials—including linoleum blocks, egg cartons, takeout containers, foam, string, screens, and even food—to create an endless number of prints. Prints can be made in multiples, but because they're handmade they can still be very personal.

Materials
↪ Tracing paper
↪ Fine-tip permanent marker
↪ Linoleum block
↪ Paper
↪ Pencil
↪ Block printing ink
↪ Card stock

Tools
↪ Linoleum cutting tool
↪ Ink tray
↪ Brayer

Artist bio
↪ Charlie and Sarah Adams are Brooklyn-based designer/makers who run an online shop that specializes in handmade T-shirts, notecards, soaps, and apparel.

01 Begin by sketching your image onto tracing paper using a fine-tip permanent marker. It's useful to sketch onto tracing paper, as block printing uses inverted images.

02 Make a photocopy of your sketch. Make sure to flip the image if you intend to do a direct image transfer. If you would rather use copy paper to transfer the image, place the image on the copier with the ink side facing up.

03 To do a direct image transfer, make sure that the image reflects the position of the original subject. Choose your lino block. Blocks vary greatly, and with a little practice you will determine which you prefer. Our preference is for lino blocks with wooden backs. These can be hard to carve and your blade can slip easily, so we recommend placing them on a heater to warm them up before carving. We have used a Speedball Speedy-Cut printing block for this workthrough, which is extremely easy to cut from.

04 Flip the copy and place it onto the carving block. Using pencil strokes, cover the entire back surface of the image evenly. This is an amazing magic trick that will impress.

05 Lift the paper to reveal the transferred image— it should be a mirror image of the original. If you feel the lines are too faint you can use a fine-tip permanent marker to trace over them.

06 Carve the image out of the block using the cutting tool. Start with wider blades to cover more surface areas and switch to smaller blades for areas of detail. Think about what you want your final image to look like. For this print we carved away the teapot and left the outline and background raised for printing.

07 Pour some ink into a tray and roll your brayer through it. Roll the ink evenly until you hear it smacking or sticking. This is a sign that it's ready to use. Roll the ink evenly onto your carved block, again listening for the sticking sound. Once complete, remove any excess ink from the carved image.

08 Take a blank card and place it on top of the inked block. Press the card evenly and firmly over the image. Your first card won't usuallly look great, but after a few layers of ink the block will become much more print-friendly. Remove the card from the block to reveal the image, and allow to dry for 24–48 hours. The ink is meant to be sticky and slow-drying, so it needs a longer drying time than acrylic or tempera paint. Make sure the prints are separated and not stacked together.

WOODBLOCK PRINTING:
Sarah Keehan

I developed an interest in letterpress and typography when I was undertaking a graphic design degree, and always made typography a key element of my illustrations. I wanted to make a children's story about a boy who talked too much, and felt this was a great opportunity to include lots of fun, playful type. I love the textures you can get from using woodblock type, and really enjoy the hands-on process and immediate results you can achieve using this technique.

Materials
➪ Pencil
➪ Sketchbook
➪ Letterpress ink
➪ Paper

Tools
➪ Woodblock type
➪ Spatula
➪ Flat surface (such as metal or glass)
➪ Brayer

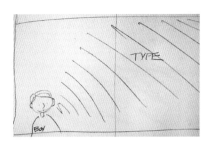

01 I always like to plan my images by doing a rough pencil drawing in a sketchbook before I begin. I like to have a general idea of where the different elements are going to go on the page. It means I know what I'm going to need when it comes to printing the type and allows me to save time when laying things out on the computer.

02 Letterpress printing normally involves a lot of preparatory work, such as setting the type and securing it in a frame. However, for this project I knew I would be scanning my prints and doing a lot of the layout work on computer, so once I had chosen the letters to use I was ready to start printing.

03 Letterpress ink is used in much the same way as linoprinting ink, and is available at many art supply stores. Use a spatula to scoop the ink out of the tin and onto a flat surface (preferably metal or glass), ink up your brayer, and roll evenly over the surface of the letters.

04 Lay your paper down on a flat surface and push each letter down onto the page. This process is much like potato printing. The first print tends not to be great because the letters are so inky, but you can reuse the letters several times without needing to ink up again. The longer you leave the letters, the more texture you will get on your prints.

05 Remember not to be too worried about where each letter goes, as you will be able to scan your work and rearrange the letters later on. Overlapping the type can sometimes produce interesting results, as demonstrated above. It's fun to experiment, and even if you don't use all of your prints in the final project, you may well use them for other projects.

06 Once you've finished printing, scan your prints and import them into Photoshop. From here you can select the letters individually, enabling you to move the type around freely and experiment with different layouts. For this project, I wanted the letters to fit well together, almost like a jigsaw puzzle.

07 I wanted to use my type in a children's picture book, so I drew my boy character by hand, scanned the drawing, and then retouched it in Photoshop. Finally, I combined the illustration with the type to create my finished piece.

Artist bio
↪ Sarah Keehan is a designer and children's book illustrator. She is based in Dublin, Ireland.

3D

In the twenty-first century, design and illustration have developed well beyond the printed page. This is evidenced in the increase of design-conscious plush toys, handmade books, paper craft, and even the new phenomenon known as "guerrilla knitting." There has also been an increase in large home furnishing companies commissioning illustrators to develop soft furnishings, kitchenware, and ceramics, and fashion designers using the work of artists and illustrators in their collections.

Designers are creating unique handmade goods for a growing market that doesn't want to dress or fill their home with off-the-peg, mass-produced items. In this market, independent designer/makers provide a refreshing, localized alternative.

In keeping with this ideal, this chapter includes work from Naomi Avsec, who started her career selling from a stall at the fashionable Spitalfields Market in London. Naomi went on to collaborate with Paul Smith, embroidering a series of suede shoes with old-fashioned brogue patterns, creating a fresh and new take on a timeless classic design (see page 104).

1

Ashley Thomas is another independent designer/maker who has created her own collections alongside working as a freelance surface designer for many major clients. Ashley has always retained a very illustrative approach to her work, which includes cushions, greeting cards, prints, and wallpapers (see page 123). Her quirky, eclectic imagery is applied across a range of functional objects, adding a level of individuality that can rarely be found in even the most progressive of chain stores.

There are also a growing number of designers making their own books using traditional bookbinding methods. Rejecting high-tech, modern printing methods, each book, by the very nature of its construction, is unique and individualized, celebrating its handcrafted materiality. Julie Smith Schneider, aka Your Secret Admiral, creates sketchbooks and notebooks made out of recycled paper and found materials; the covers are collaged with new and old found imagery. The results are unique handmade books free from the dehumanization of mass production; a new book with character and a sense of the past (see page 122).

Another trend in 3D graphics has been the rise in popularity of plush toys aimed at adults and children alike. This chapter showcases hand-knitted plush toys made by Anne Brassier, with each having its own unique name, characteristics, and quirks (see page 98). The influence of myths and monsters has also made its mark on the worlds of design and illustration, and Phil Barbato is one such graphic designer who makes plush toy monsters that are cute and comical (see page 99). The influx of character design is a refreshing antidote to the often serious, chin-rubbing design world. Plush toys combine good design with light-heartedness and humor, with no function other than simply to be enjoyed.

Somewhat related to this resurgence of traditional craft methods is guerrilla knitting. Creating what has been termed as "knitted graffiti," these knits customize and adorn everything from landmarks to the everyday mundane. It's anarchy with irony. These knitters are out there breaking the law by spreading the world with knitted loveliness!

Finally, Dan McPharlin is an artist who doesn't fit into any neat category. He creates miniature handmade paper sculptures of music analogue equipment. The lo-fi subject matter represents a time when musicmaking was less slick and digital, and likewise, the very construction of the miniature sculptures reflects this ethos, using nothing but card and glue and constructed by hand. They have even gained the attention of the press, being featured on the cover of *Wallpaper** (see pages 116–117).

The work featured in this chapter is embodied in the series of four tutorials included at the end of the chapter, which demonstrate how to make a plush toy, paint a pair of shoes, make an illustrative embroidery, and bind a book. I hope these tutorials will inspire you to make your own innovative 3D creations!

3

4

Anne Brassier

After graduating from the University of Stirling in Scotland, Anne moved to London to work for the award-winning design studio, Airside. You can find Stitches, her wool creations, in the Airside shop, where they have achieved legendary status.

1–2 Taking inspiration from Japanese handmade toys, Anne's hand-knitted Stitches creatures are made from wool and plastic. Each Stitches creature appears physically (and emotionally) damaged, and their journeys are as varied as their personalities. Each Stitch is looking for a new home where it can be nurtured and rehabilitated, and comes in its own travel box with an adoption certificate.

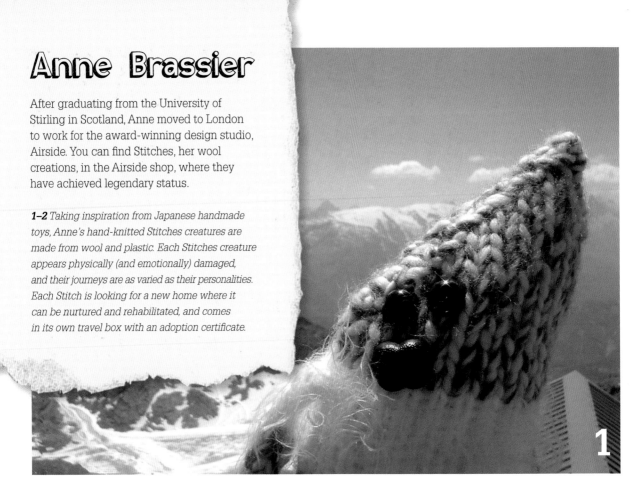

Phil Barbato

Phil Barbato studied sculpture and extended media at Virginia Commonwealth University, USA, and now works from his home studio as a part-time web designer and plush toymaker in Richmond, Virginia. His favorite material to work with when making his toys is faux fur. As well as selling on Etsy, Phil also sells his toys at craft fairs across the USA. (See pages 124–125 for Phil's plush toy workthrough.)

1–2 A selection of Phil's plush toy monsters sewn by hand and machine using fleece and faux fur.

1

2

Ethan Park

After studying publishing and computer graphics at Tongmyong University of Information Technology in South Korea, Ethan moved to the UK to undertake an MA in communications at Kingston University. He works on a range of web, motion graphics, print, font, and installation projects, as well as working at Virgin Records UK as a freelance designer. Ethan's real passion is typography, and his work is experimental and often uses unorthodox materials, such as type made out of bread. He has been recognized in many international design competitions, including winning a merit award at the 84th New York Art Directors Club. He was also a finalist in the 2005 International Output Students Competition and a finalist in the Moscow International Biennale of Golden Bee 6.

1, 3, 4 These three pieces were created for Ethan's final MA assessment. Titled "Marry Me," the project allowed Ethan to communicate aspects of his personality to a public audience in a simple and candid way. Each visual message features handcrafted typography that has been incorporated into a book. Image 1 (What If…) was made using leaves, and implies that Ethan is a good thinker; image 3 (No Days Off) was made by applying masking tape to a tree, and implies that Ethan is a hard worker; and image 4 (See You) uses symbols and printed images pinned to Ethan's clothes, and was used as a promotional poster for the project.
2 This is a still from an online video titled Don't Feed the Pigeons, *which was made with pieces of bread and black tape affixed to the pavement.*

1

2

3

Kate Lyons

Kate Lyons studied at Central Saint Martins College of Art & Design in London and then went on to do a placement in London with Thomas Matthews design agency and REG Design in London. As this drew to an end, Phil Baines, who had been her tutor at college, asked Kate to design an artist's book with him, and since then she has found herself (somewhat unexpectedly) freelancing from her home studio. Kate's favorite medium is print, and she has a special love for books. Kate has been featured in a number of publications, including *Tactile: High Touch Visuals* and *Playful Type*.

1–2 This handbound book was made for Kate's degree dissertation. Sections of the dissertation were printed on different paper stock and bound together with pink thread.
3 Anyone could make a handstitched badge and add it to this tree. Many of the badges didn't make sense separately, but they all came together to build a larger, cohesive image.
4 This cross-stitch of a Blue Tit was Kate's entry for the Nationwide Mercury Prize Art Competition.

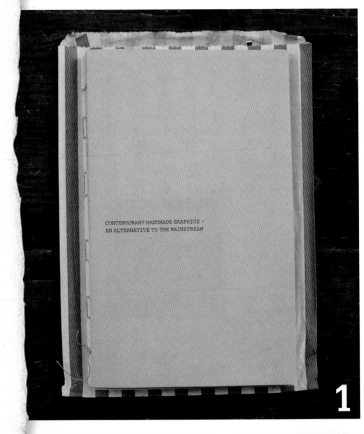

1

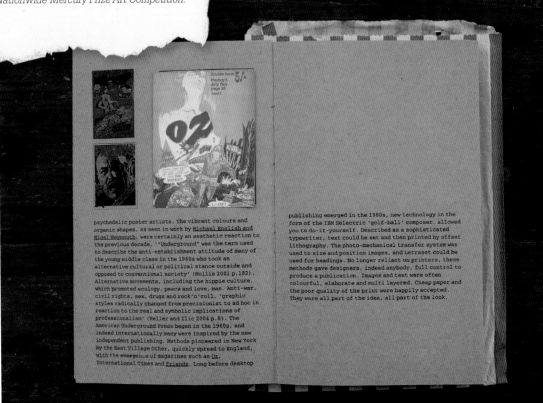

2

Naomi Avsec

Since graduating from Chelsea College of Art & Design in London, Naomi has exhibited her paintings both locally in the UK as well as internationally. Inspired largely by artists such as Paula Rego and Ana Maria Pacheco, her twisted visions have forged a distinct and individual illustrative language. Alongside painting, Naomi also works as a freelance textile embroiderer, and has completed commissions for a number of British fashion designers, including Paul Smith and Nicole Farhi, as well as for Liberty in London.

1 Naomi uses a sewing machine to doodle, letting her imagination shape each piece. Shown here are a selection of embroidered samples, including intricate lettering and illustrations.
2 Embroidered brogue boots designed for Paul Smith's Paul x collection.

1

2

1

Knit Sea

Elina Arpiainen, aka Knit Sea, was the first guerrilla knitter to bring the movement to attention in her home country of Finland, and has since inspired others to take up the trend. She even made it onto the Finnish news with a short documentary about her work. Knit Sea has been included in numerous exhibitions and has been featured in newspapers and magazines. Her goal is to continue spreading the word about guerrilla knitting.

1–2 A series of knitted wool creations left in public spaces.

2

Jaco Haasbroek

Jaco Haasbroek studied fine art at Stellenbosch University in South Africa. He lives in Cape Town, where he works for an advertising agency, as well as having a studio close to his home where most of his plush toys are created. Jaco loves drawing, and his ideas often begin in his sketchbook. One of Jaco's career highlights has been having a design selected and printed by T-shirt company Threadless.

1–7 Jaco's plush toys are made using felt and polyester filling. Many of his toys are influenced by music and are based on a particular song or band member, such as image 4, which is based on Thom Yorke, and image 6, which is based on Sam Eastgate from the band Late of the Pier. Other creatures are based on shapes or animals (see images 2 and 5).

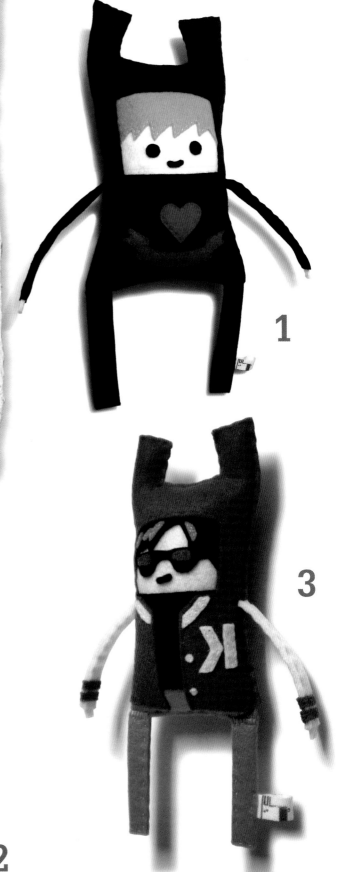

1

3

2

4

5

6

7

Hiutwig

Hiutwig is a Brazilian illustrator who is studying communications at the Federal University of Rio de Janeiro. As a child, Hiutwig was put off art by traditional drawing methods, but has since managed to forget all the rules and develop her own unique drawing style. In her own words, Hiutwig likes to keep things "crooked and colorful," and is inspired by the work of Jon Burgerman (see pages 24–25), Ricardo Siri Liniers, and Yoshitomo Nara. (See pages 126–127 for Hiutwig's painted sneakers workthrough.)

1 & 3 *Examples of Hiutwig's doodles and illustrations that she makes to give away to friends or as gifts to her customers.*
2 *This illustration was drawn directly onto a pink T-shirt using blue fabric markers.*
4 *This pair of canvas ballerina slip-on shoes were created using only fabric markers.*
5 *These baby sneakers (also illustrated using fabric markers) were commissioned as a present for someone's granddaughter. Because the shoes were so small, Hiutwig had to carefully plan what would work well on the shoe surface.*
6 *A pair of commissioned sneakers influenced by comic books, and made using acrylics, Sharpie markers, and fabric markers.*

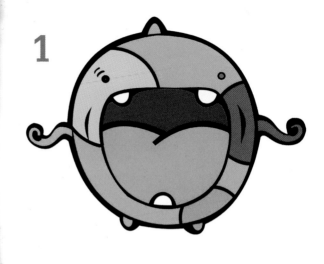

1

3

2

LOWE EVERYBODY

4

5

6

1

2

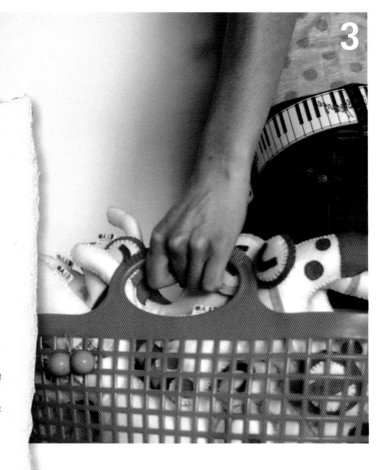

3

Claudia Carieri

Claudia Carieri is a Milan-based graphic designer and illustrator. Claudia studied fine art before specializing in advertising and graphic design, and has also illustrated a coloring book for De Agostini. Claudia makes plush toys by hand alongside her design and illustration work, which she sells in her online store.

1–4 These plush monster dolls are made by hand using felt. Claudia usually scribbles out her design on paper before cutting out the felt pieces. Each monster takes approximately half an hour to make.

Pixelgarten

Pixelgarten is a multidisciplinary design agency based in Frankfurt, Germany. It was formed by Catrin Altenbrandt and Adrian Niessler, who both studied at the Academy of Art & Design in Offenbach, Germany. Pixelgarten work for a variety of clients in the fields of illustration, fashion, corporate identity, and editorial design. They also spend their time working on self-initiated projects and are very active in exhibiting their work.

1–2 Sushi *(produced by the Art Directors Club Germany) asked Pixelgarten to create a Scout uniform out of paper for the magazine.*
3 NEON *magazine commissioned Pixelgarten to create lifesize versions of computer games, such as* Tetris, The Sims, *and* Super Mario. *The pieces were made using paper, cardboard, foam board, and boxes. (Photographed by Markus Burke and Roderick Eichinger.)*
4 *This piece was made for the cover of* Three D: Graphic Spaces, *published by Birkhäuser Publishing. (Photographed by Christiane Feser.)*
5 *This book cover was created for* Tactile: High Touch Visuals, *published by Die Gestalten Verlag, using paper, cardboard, and wood.*

1

2

3

4

5

Bendita Gloria

Alba Rosell and Santi Fuster formed the Barcelona-based graphic design studio Bendita Gloria after meeting at ESDi (the Higher School of Design) in Barcelona. Bendita Gloria received gold and silver at the Laus Awards in 2009 (an initiative of ADG-FAD, the Laus Awards set the standard for design and visual communication in Spain) and gold and bronze at the European Design Awards in 2009.

1 *This two-poster series was created using hama beads mounted on wood boards.*
2 *This set of promotional materials was created for Bendita Gloria's exhibition at the FAD (Fostering Arts and Design) gallery in Barcelona. Each piece was handsewn with thread onto card.*
3 *This poster was created for a fashion store using a cross-stitching method.*

1

Actes de fe.
Gràfica i autoproducció.

UNA
EXPO
HI-TECH

Del 9 al 20 de juny a la Cripta del FAD
Plaça dels Àngels, 5-6 (Barcelona)

Inauguració: dilluns 9 de juny a les 20.00h

Alba Rosell
www.benditagloria.com

Organitza: Col·labora:

2

3

Dan McPharlin

Dan studied visual arts at the University of South Australia and works from his home studio on the South Australian coast as a freelance artist and web designer. Dan started his career by experimenting with cardboard as a sculptural medium, which eventually led him to develop miniature music analogue equipment. One of his career highlights so far has included designing the cover of *Wallpaper** magazine.

1 Produced for an exhibition at The Museum of Contemporary Art, Chicago. Materials used include mat board, paper, and cord.
2 Produced for an Esquire magazine photoshoot. Materials used include mat board, paper, and plastic sheeting.
3 Produced for the Mr. Chop Sounds from the Cave 12in EP. Materials used include mat board, paper, plastic sheeting, and cord.

1

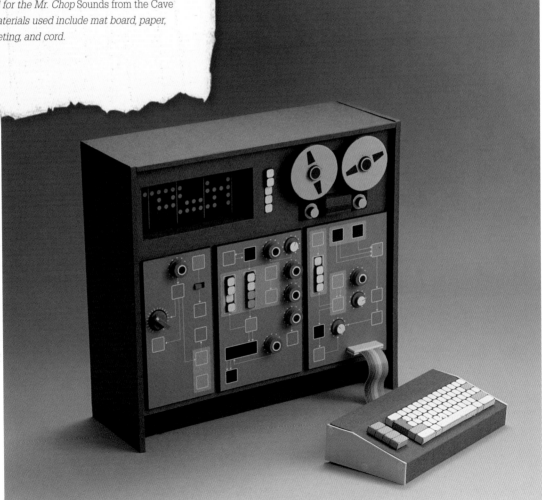

2

3

Gluekit

Gluekit are made up of Christopher and Kathleen Sleboda. Christopher began drawing and sketching from a very early age. In high school he got into the punk scene by creating zines, and then in the early 1990s started a successful T-shirt and music mail order business. Kathleen grew up in San Francisco, where her love of creative expression, craft, and color began. Christopher and Kathleen met at Yale University and went on to form illustration and design agency Gluekit, which is based in New Haven, Connecticut. Together, they have developed very distinct ways of conceptually approaching projects that are unique and unexpected. In 2007, Gluekit launched a successful project named Part of It, which strives to raise awareness about issues in a smart, visually stimulating, and graphic way.

1–3 These pieces were created for PRINT *magazine's December 2008 Regional Design Annual. The images reference a designer's toolkit, and play with repeated motifs of shape, color, and perspective to create a suite of staged typographic scenes. Gluekit constructed the round shapes with hula hoops and the rest of the shapes using wooden frames that were then covered with brightly colored felt. Other materials used include styrofoam, spray paint, and tape.*

1

2

3

Annika Koski

Annika Koski is originally from Finland but studied fashion at the National College of Art and Design in Dublin, Ireland. After graduating, Annika was spotted by John Rocha (a Hong Kong-born fashion designer based in Ireland), who offered her a job creating graphics for his fashion label. After a number of years she set up as a freelance graphic designer and illustrator. Her career highlights so far include completing an exhibition called "Contagious Creativity" for the Science Gallery in Dublin, a collaborative project featuring jazz music, digital visuals, and large handmade/drawn illustrations. Her work has been published in *Analogue Magazine* and she has also worked for many clients in the music industry.

1–2 Experimental typography made using LEGO®. The pieces were made for Out Of Site, a program run by The Dublin Fringe Festival that provides a platform for artists to create innovative performative work in public spaces. The pieces were used across a range of platforms, including leaflets, posters, and the Out Of Site website.
3 This piece was created for Could Be Me, a project where international artists visually interpret the same sentence (see couldbe.me). This piece was created with LEGO® pieces constructed on a wooden floor.

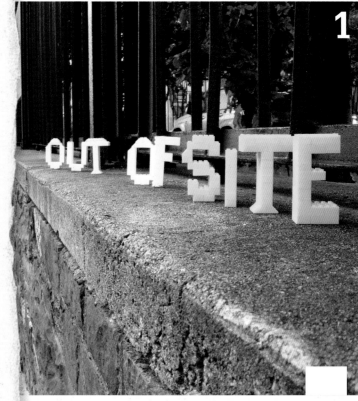

1

2

3

Your Secret Admiral

After receiving a Bachelor of Fine Art from Virginia Commonwealth University in Richmond, Julie S. Schneider (Your Secret Admiral) moved to Brooklyn to begin her creative career. She began selling her handmade books, drawings, and paper goods under the name Your Secret Admiral on Etsy during her last year of university, and eventually began working fulltime for Etsy. Most of Julie's products are environmentally friendly and created from recycled, reused, rescued, or salvaged materials. Julie's favorite medium to work with is paper, but she also loves using fabric, thread, and ink.

1 This book is from Your Secret Admiral's series of Ultimate Sketchbooks, in which Julie explores combinations of materials to make a multifunctional sketchbook. This book incorporates a cutting mat as its cover.
2 This journal was made using the cover of a discarded book.
3 This travel journal features an illustration of a suitcase-wielding couple, and the inside is interspersed with airmail envelopes that travel documentation and ephemera can be tucked into.

1

2

3

Ashley Thomas

Ashley Thomas studied surface pattern design at Staffordshire University in the UK, and now lives and works in Derbyshire. After graduating in 2007, Ashley took part in a graduate show where she made some fantastic contacts. This allowed her to embark on a freelance career working for a variety of companies designing greeting cards, canvases, and fashion prints. Ashley launched her own collection of wallpapers, prints, cushions, purses, and greeting cards in 2008, which are available from a selection of stockists in the UK and France. Ashley has also worked on a freelance basis for a range of companies, including Mamas & Papas, Foliage Inc., and Juna Clothing.

1 & 3 Titled Plug it In, this series of cushions was inspired by animals and science. Ashley created the initial artwork on paper using pen, pencil, and collage. She then scanned and retouched the artwork in Photoshop, and digitally printed onto linen before sewing into cushion covers.
2 & 4 Produced in the same way, this series of cushions is titled La La Lucy, and was inspired by botanics and nature.

1

2

3

4

PLUSH TOY:
Phil Barbato

The ape plush toy in this tutorial is named Petit Chou. She was the first toy I made using long-pile faux fur. I had made ape toys previously with different fabrics and over time developed a style and shape that I liked. I love these little guys. They're soft and happy, and their eyes, faces, and bellies are a blast to make. I always smile when I turn them the right side out for the first time.

Materials
- Long-pile faux fur
- Fleece
- Felt
- Craft foam rubber
- Thread
- Polyfil stuffing

Tools
- Fabric scissors
- Sewing machine
- Pins
- Sewing needle
- Tailor's chalk

01 The first thing I do is choose a color for the long-pile faux fur. You should be able to buy faux fur at most fabric stores, or alternatively online. I have chosen deep purple for this project.

02 For the main body, cut out two large matching rectangles from the faux fur. Cut out the face and belly areas from the fleece and the facial features and belly button from the felt. I also use fleece for the eye circles, but find felt is better for the smaller details.

03 Sew the felt features to the fleece face and belly sections by hand using needle and thread. Cut the teeth out of the craft foam—I have made Petit Chou's teeth irregular rather than straight. Fold over the fleece and insert the teeth in place, and then sew straight across using a sewing machine.

04 Pin the fleece face and belly to one of the faux fur rectangles and sew them on closely around the edges to the shape you require. Carefully trim around the face and belly with fabric scissors.

05 At this stage I also draw the final shape around one of my rectangles with tailor's chalk and then with the sewing machine. Trim around the shape, lay on top of the other rectangle, and trim to match. This makes it easier to sew and prevents the fur from getting caught.

06 Pin the two bodies together with the fur sides facing each other and sew around the edges. Leave an opening 4–6in/10–15cm at the bottom of the body, as this is what you will use to insert the stuffing.

07 Trim off any of the excess faux fur and turn the body inside out. Insert the polyfil stuffing through the hole and carefully sew it up using a sewing machine or needle and thread. Now your little ape toy is born! Ain't she a peach?

Artist bio
⇨Phil Barbato is a part-time web designer and artist based in Richmond, Virginia. More of his work can be seen on page 99.

PAINTED SNEAKERS:
Hiutwig

I like drawing on physical objects more than on paper or canvas. To me, objects don't seem to put as much pressure on you to make something special and pretty. A friend once suggested that I should paint on sneakers, which I thought was a really nice idea, because plain white shoes can sometimes use a little cheering up. I also like the idea of drawing onto something that I am going to walk around in and that other people will see.

Materials
⇨ White canvas sneakers
⇨ Pencil
⇨ Eraser
⇨ Square paintbrush
⇨ Round paintbrush
⇨ Fabric paint
⇨ Fabric marker pens
⇨ Permanent marker pens
⇨ Waterproof spray
⇨ Shoelaces

02 I usually link both sneakers as a pair through the use of color and detail. I don't like to make both shoes identical, but they should at least look like they belong together, so it's ok to repeat some elements in both shoes in order to make the sneakers a coherent pair.

01 Using a pencil (in my case a 0.9mm Pentel mechanical pencil), draw directly onto one of the sneakers. Try not to draw too hard or it will be difficult to erase if you make a mistake. I don't usually make a sketch of the design on paper first, I just doodle all over the shoe. If it doesn't look good I erase the image and start over; however, you may prefer to sketch out your design first.

03 After all the lines have been drawn in pencil, use a small square brush and cover the larger areas (such as the tongue of the shoe) with fabric paint. Use a smaller round brush for painting on difficult spots, like the corners of the sneaker and the areas next to the pencil lines. Try not to cover the lines though; leave a small gap between the lines and the paint.

04 Use the fabric marker pens to color the small and detailed areas, trying again not to cover the pencil lines. Because the marker ink is liquid it tends to blend easily, especially if it's brand new, so use different colors to paint areas that aren't continuous. Leave a safe gap and allow a couple of hours for the marker ink to fully dry up.

07 Outline the smaller areas, such as facial expressions, teeth, and small lettering, using a marker with a very fine tip. I tend to use a brand new marker specifically for these kinds of outlines as it creates a more dynamic effect.

05 I next colored some of the remaining blank areas as soon as the colored sections were dry. When you have a fully colored pair of shoes with tiny white outlines, leave the shoes to dry again, this time a little longer than before.

06 Fill in the white outlines using a permanent or fabric marker. Because of the nature of the marker ink, don't take too long filling in the lines otherwise the outline color will bleed. Trace the lines with steady and fast moves, or use a permanent marker with a slightly less liquid ink, such as a Sharpie marker.

08 Once the outlines are finished, the painting is almost complete. In order to extend the longevity of the painting and make the shoes easier to clean, coat them evenly with a waterproof spray.

09 After waterproofing, the only thing left to add is the laces. Keeping in mind the already colorful sneakers you could go with plain white laces, but I've chosen to use fluorescent yellow in this case because it's my favorite color! (See the final result opposite.)

Artist bio
⇨ Hiutwig is a Bazillian-based illustrator. More of her work can be seen on pages 108–109.

ILLUSTRATIVE EMBROIDERY:
Mithila Shafiq

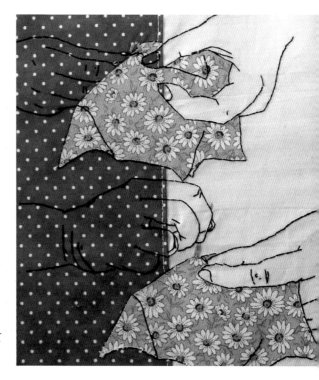

This piece originally came out of a reportage project I was doing. I was at my local Stitch 'n Bitch group and started taking photos of the ladies crafting. I was especially enamored by their hands and ended up using them as reference photos for future drawings. When it came to designing this piece, I really wanted to incorporate the craft itself somehow. Looking through my images of crafters, I found several that involved sewing using needle and thread. I've always loved the soft-textured quality embroidery gives to line drawings, so bringing the two together I developed my "metabroidery" embroidery!

Materials
⇨ Paper
⇨ Pencil
⇨ Neutral-colored fabric (cotton or linen)
⇨ Tracing paper
⇨ Patterned fabric
⇨ Fusible webbing
⇨ Water-soluble embroidery fabric
⇨ Thread
⇨ Sponge

Tools
⇨ Fabric scissors
⇨ Sewing machine
⇨ Sewing needle
⇨ Tailor's chalk or marker
⇨ Pins

 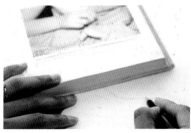 

01 Begin by sourcing your image. I went to my local Stitch 'n Bitch group and spent time taking photographs of the crafty ladies and their hands. It's far more interesting (and sociable) than downloading images from the web (and you're also less likely to come up against copyright issues!).

02 Pick a photo you're happy with and scale it to the desired size. Print a copy and then draw your image from it. At this stage you will need to tweak the image in order to make it more about what you want to show.

03 Cut your fabric a couple of inches larger than your embroidery hoop. Stretch the fabric over your embroidery hoop and secure it in place. Trace your drawing and use this to decide how it is going to sit within the hoop. Mark the edge of the hoop on the fabric lightly with a pencil as a guide.

04 Decide how you want to incorporate the patterned pieces of fabric into your embroidery. For example, if your drawing includes a piece of "fabric" that the hands are embroidering, then use this. Otherwise, use a simple geometric shape cut with pinking shears to give it some interest.

05 Trace your "fabric" or shape onto some tracing paper and cut it out. Turn the tracing paper piece upside down and trace around it on the greaseproof paper backing of the fusible webbing.

06 Cut around the fusible webbing and iron it (greaseproof paper side up) to the back of the patterned fabric. Once cool, carefully cut out the shape and peel off the greaseproof paper backing.

07 Take the neutral fabric out of the hoop and, using your traced image as a guide, place your patterned fabric where you want it to go.

08 Iron the patterned fabric onto the neutral fabric. Once cool, return the whole piece into the hoop and secure it, keeping the hoop-tightening fastener at the top.

09 If you are using the water-soluble embroidery fabric, trace your image onto it, arrange it on the hoop, and pin it down. Water-soluble embroidery fabric dissolves under water after the embroidery is finished, so it's ideal for a project like this. If you haven't got any water-soluble embroidery fabric, there is nothing stopping you from drawing directly with a light pencil straight onto the fabric, or tracing it out in some other way.

10 Stitch, stitch, stitch! Choose some embroidery thread (black, dark gray, or brown work best) and start using a simple running or backstitch to sew your image. You can add interest by using different colored thread to fill in the thread and needle sections of the image.

11 Once you've finished sewing, tie off the ends and tidy up any stray threads. Use a damp sponge to melt away the water-soluble embroidery fabric. If you feel it needs it, take the piece out of the hoop and give it a gentle hand-wash and dry (only do this if your fabrics and threads are colorfast though!). If the piece has become creased or is looking a little untidy, give it a quick iron.

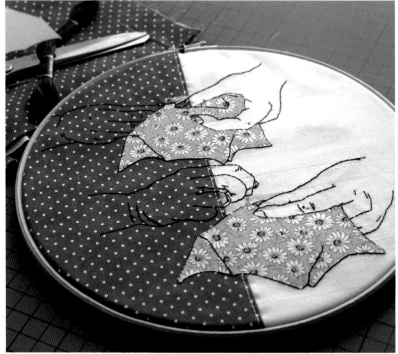

12 Put the piece of fabric back into the hoop, turn it upside down, and using a large running stitch, sew around the edge of the fabric. Pull it tight and tie it off.

13 Now you're all done and can hang your piece of embroidery art from the metal fastener on the hoop.

Artist bio
→ Mithila Shafiq is a UK-based freelance illustrator.

BOOKBINDING:
Your Secret Admiral

In this tutorial I will show you how to make a do-si-do book. Like the basic step used in square dancing where two partners pivot around each other, a do-si-do book swings between two signatures. They are almost like two books in one, and are excellent for dual purposes, such as drawings and notes. Follow this workthrough and you'll be whipping up your own books in no time!

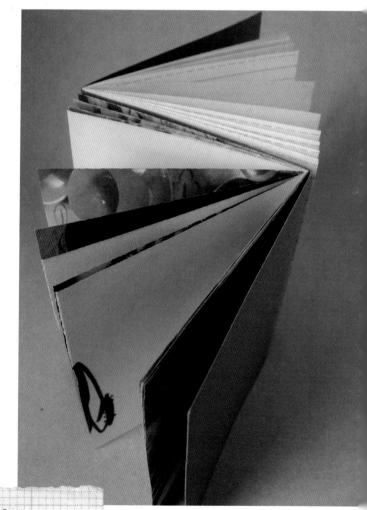

Basic terms
- ⇨ Signature: a gathering of folded pages
- ⇨ Bone folder: a bookbinding tool used for scoring and creasing paper
- ⇨ Awl: a bookbinding tool used for punching holes in paper and covers

Tools
- ⇨ Scissors
- ⇨ Guillotine (optional)
- ⇨ Bone folder
- ⇨ Awl

Materials
- ⇨ Notepaper
- ⇨ Sturdy paper or cardboard
- ⇨ Ruler
- ⇨ Pencil
- ⇨ Needle
- ⇨ Linen thread

01 I began by preparing the two signatures and covers. To make each signature, fold 5–10 sheets of paper in half and trim them to the size you require. Choose a sturdy paper or lightweight cardboard for the covers. Cut them with scissors or a guillotine to the same height as one of the signatures and three times as wide as one signature. Fold the cover into thirds using a bone folder tool so it forms a "Z" shape.

02 Before you start on your book, make a sample signature using a single piece of paper that is the same height and width as your signatures.

03 Using a ruler, measure and mark the placement for three holes on the sample signature with pencil—you'll use this as a guide for making holes in your real signatures and covers. Put one signature into one of the folds of the Z-shaped cover. Using a bookbinder's awl and your sample signature as a guide, punch three holes through each signature and the cover.

04 Thread your needle with the linen thread and pull it through the center of the first signature, leaving a tail of thread a couple of inches long inside the signature.

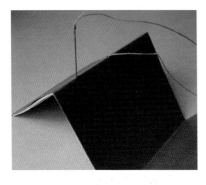

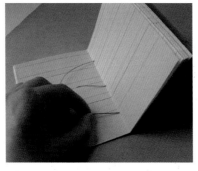

05 Push the needle through the top hole on the spine of your book.

06 Pull the needle through the bottom hole on the inside of your book, skipping over the center hole and thread tail.

07 Pull the needle through the center hole on the outside of the book, making sure that the needle and thread is on one side of the long center stitch and the thread tail is on the other.

08 Remove the needle and trim the threads. Pull each thread taut to even out the tension of the stitching.

09 Tie a simple knot over the long center stitch and trim the excess thread.

10 Repeat steps 1–8 on the second signature, and your do-si-do book is complete.

Artist bio
⇨ Your Secret Admiral is a US-based artist and handmade bookmaker. More of her work can be found on page 122.

MIXED-
MEDIA
COLLAGE

The word collage originates from the French words *papiers collés* and *découpage*, which are used to describe the method of sticking cut paper onto a surface. Much like its original meaning, collage is still used to describe the techniques and resulting works of art in which pieces of paper, photographs, fabric, and other media are arranged and stuck down to a surface. It has been used since the early twentieth century and continues to be a valuable technique among artists and designers today.

Using combined media can be a perfect way of creating an interesting sense of pictorial space, such as contrasting photographs with patterns, painting, and drawing. Collage also allows the designer or artist to incorporate historical images with those collected when traveling or with material from everyday life. For example, at the end of this chapter illustrator and printmaker Jim Butler demonstrates how to create a collaged drawing on location using imagery from his journeys and daily life (see pages 166–167). Collage is a perfect medium for juxtaposing eclectic imagery and different image making methods, and often leads the artist into unexpected and interesting new ways of working.

1 By Kate Slater, see pages 140–141.
2 By Chen Ying-Tzu (Hazen Chen), see pages 146–147 and 168–171.
3 By Grady McFerrin, see pages 144–145.
4 By Hardland/Heartland, see pages 148–149.
5 By Jodie Hurt, see pages 158–159.

1

2

If I can be a stone, I will protect you without any weapon. In fact, I am a weakness one, nothing I can do just watch you like an infant.

Craig Atkinson is an artist who uses a combination of drawing, collage, and paint, often with found imagery from popular and contemporary culture. Images of the British monarchy are used alongside celebrities and are often humorously defaced. Craig also combines this imagery with collaged elements of paintings and drawings (see page 138).

Using materials more often seen in the elementary school art room, Hayley Lock uses stickers, glitter, and sequins on found imagery and postcard reproductions of old masters' portraits, resulting in familiar icons of art history suddenly being shifted into a new context. This intriguing mixture of throwaway, childlike craft materials and high culture examines different elements of culture, status, and iconography (see pages 154–155).

Collage is, by its very nature, a perfect medium if you are interested in combining otherwise incongruous imagery in a quirky and eclectic way. Robert Hope's work is an ideal example of this, combining found imagery with hand-drawn type (see pages 142–143).

Grady McFerrin has taken a slightly different approach, creating 3D collages within a frame using wood and found and hand-drawn imagery. His collages play on an interesting use of space, blurring the boundaries between sculpture and illustration (see pages 144–145). Children's book illustrator Kate Slater also uses the technique of layering collage, and even hanging imagery like a mobile, photographing it, and turning it into a 2D format (see pages 140–141).

Collage is ideally suited to working in handmade sketchbooks; a technique used by artist Martha Rich. Martha takes imagery from the 1970s as her starting point, and then uses pen and paint to combine eclectic, lateral imagery. Her use of overwash color and type is especially strong, forming a disjointed, visually powerful narrative (see pages 156–157).

Four tutorials are also included at the end of this chapter, taking you step-by-step through each practitioner's creative decisions. I hope they provide a valuable insight into a variety of techniques and methods used in collage, and inspire you to create your own unique work.

Craig Atkinson

Craig Atkinson studied fine art at Leeds Metropolitan University in the UK. Since graduating he has developed a successful career working as an artist and illustrator for numerous magazines, as well as exhibiting and selling his work locally and internationally. Craig runs an online business called Café Royal, which specializes in artists' books and zines, and also works as a part-time university lecturer.

1 This piece is from an ongoing series of bearded ladies, with a particular focus on royals and C-list celebrities. The eyes were blocked out in this piece and a beard was drawn, like those often doodled in school textbooks.
2 This piece is from one of Craig's sketchbooks. His sketchbooks are very spontaneous, and are the starting point for most of his work.
3 This is from a series of puppets based on famous people in disguise. This one is of Frida Kahlo, Mexican warrior.

1

3

2

Marin
van Uhm

Marin van Uhm was born in Groningen in the Netherlands. She studied at the École Nationale Supérieure d'Arts Appliqués, Olivier de Serres in Paris, where she now lives and works. Marin's favorite way of working is by hand. She is constantly inspired by the city of Paris, and its wealth of exhibitions, libraries, and lectures. Marin's ambition is to set up her own design agency.

1–2 This alphabet was created as part of a research project based on the motto of Europe (unie dans la diversité/unity in diversity). Marin cut various shapes out of paper and arranged them into letters on a luminous table to photograph. She was interested in looking at the ways separate elements could be harmonious.

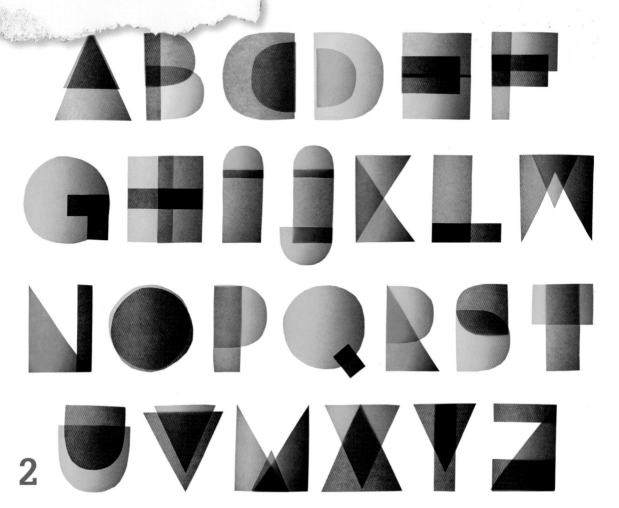

Kate Slater

Since graduating from Kingston University in London, Kate Slater has developed a successful career as a freelance illustrator. Kate works mainly in collage with a combination of paper, cutouts, and wire, which she uses to create suspended relief illustrations. Kate's clients have included Random House Children's Books, Passion Pictures, *The Guardian*, and *Amelia's Magazine*. Andersen Press will publish her first children's book in 2010.

1 *Collaged paper cutouts created for a self-initiated poster.*
2 *Suspended relief illustration created as a proof for* Magpie's Treasure, *Kate's children's picture book.*
3 *Cut paper and collaged promotional poster for a fictional record store. The text included on the poster was written by Scottish poet and writer Ivor Cutler.*

1

2

3

Robert Hope

Robert Hope studied at Bradford College
and Leeds Metropolitan University in the
UK. He now lives in West Yorkshire, where
he works as an artist from his home studio.
Robert also works part-time as a tutor for
a number of local schools and colleges, and
exhibits his installation and video-based
work as often as possible. Other than his
ambitions to further exhibit internationally,
Robert is learning to play the theme music
to *Midnight Cowboy* on the harmonica.

*1–5 A series of artworks using collaged drawings
with found imagery and text.*

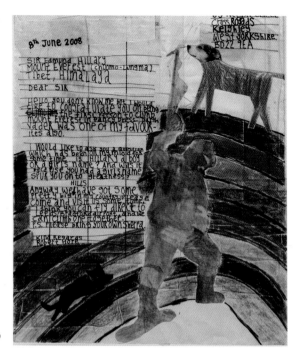

1

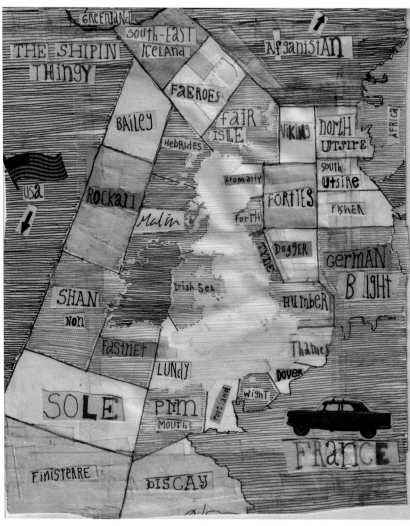

2

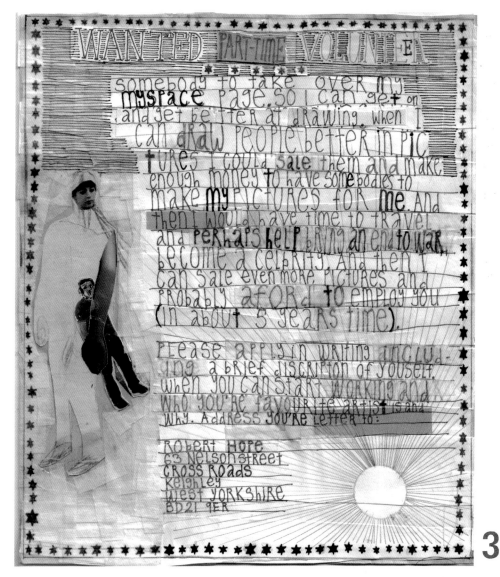

3

4

5

Grady McFerrin

Grady McFerrin studied illustration at California State University, and now lives and works in Brooklyn, New York. He is a full-time freelance illustrator, and his drawings can be seen on several wine labels, stationery products, album covers, and posters. His favorite materials to work with include shellac and pigment on vellum. Grady often uses computer editing during the final stages of his work, but is a great believer in the handmade process.

1 *This poster, created for the band My Morning Jacket, was inspired by one of their lyrics about an unfortunate man. The poster was collaged with elements found in old books and catalogs.*

2 *This diorama was created for Spirit Animals: Unlocking the Secrets of Our Animal Companions, published by Chronicle Books. The mountain areas were built out of styrofoam and white enamel paint was dripped on top of everything to create the snow scene.*

3 *This piece was also created for Spirit Animals. Grady used various photos of mountains to build the landscape in the background. The mountains in the front were constructed out of wire and papier-mâché.*

4 *This poster was created for the band The Fiery Furnaces. Hand-drawn elements were collaged with old images of stoic children.*

1

2

3

Chen Ying-Tzu (Hazen Chen)

Chen Ying-Tzu studied graphic design and design management at university. She lives in Taipei, Taiwan, and works from her home studio and as an intern at a local art studio. Chen has been interested in drawing since an early age, but it wasn't until she discovered collage that her work began to mature. She has participated in a number of exhibitions and her work has been featured on many blogs.

1 This piece was made by collaging images together to illustrate the story of a young boy trying to find his way home.
2 This collage was composed of random bits of found paper.
3 This collage incorporates hand-drawn elements that have been retouched in Photoshop. Chen took inspiration from the BBC program Animal Planet.
4 This collage incorporates a portrait from Chen's childhood, and is inpsired by the Mr. Children "Kurumi" video clip.

1

2

3

4

Hardland/ Heartland

Hardland/Heartland are a collective of artists living and working in Minneapolis. Their favorite materials to work with are paper, graphite, marker pens, paint, cloth, books, video, and computers. They are inspired by the ongoing processes and interconnectivity of their lives, and draw inspiration from each other's work. Hardland/Heartland have exhibited at the Minneapolis Institute of Arts in conjunction with the Minnesota Artist Exhibition Program. They often publish zines and have been featured in *IdN Magazine*.

1 Collage made with graphite and paint on a wooden panel.
2 Cover artwork made from paper, photocopies, graphite, and ink for Us Doves, a 45-page, full-color book produced for a Hardland/Heartland solo exhibition at the Needles and Pens gallery in San Francisco.
3 Artwork made with graphite, ink, and tape on vellum.
4 Spread from Us Doves, made with ink, paint, and paper.
5 Collage made with graphite, gouache, and a found photograph.

1

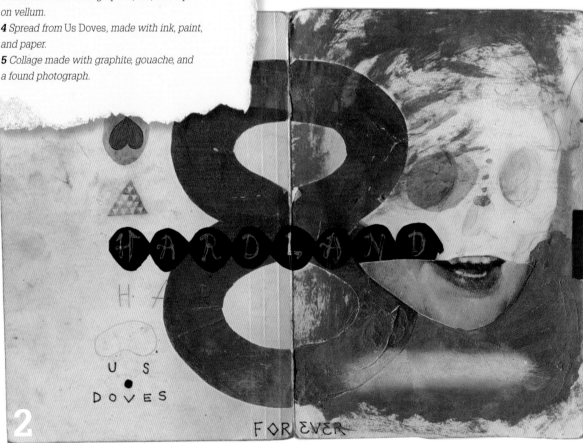

2

3

4

5

Able Parris

Able Parris studied at Rhode Island School of Design and now lives in North Carolina, where he works as a freelance designer from his home studio. Able specializes in web design, but also produces collages featuring illustration, photography, and type. One of his favorite compliments is when people tell him his work has inspired them to be more creative. Able is also a poet and has ambitions to publish a book of his collage and poetry work.

1–2 Series of collages created using various found imagery and typographic elements.

1

PLAN
PERFORM
WORRY

2

Sarah West

Sarah West studied painting at the Slade School of Fine Art in the UK and now works as an artist from her London-based studio. Her work is focused on the world of celebrities and how this relates to the history of portraiture. Sarah deconstructs celebrity magazines and takes them out of context using permanent markers. Sarah has exhibited in the UK, including the 2009 Edinburgh Annuale, and her work has been featured on the cover of *Cluster Arts Magazine*.

1–3 These artworks were created as part of the Every Tuesday *series, made using magazine cutouts and marker pens. West enjoys creating subtle visual narratives by editing and highlighting amusingly strange elements.*
4 Alongside her collage work, Sarah also paints interpretations of magazine covers. This piece, WOW Bikini!, was made with oil and acrylic on a gessoed canvas panel.

1

2

3

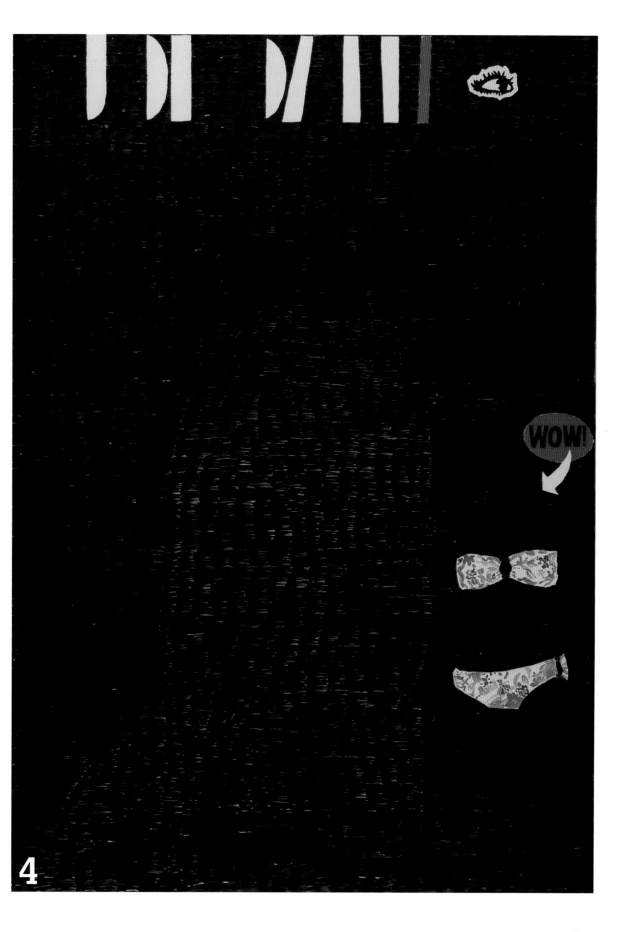

4

Hayley Lock

Hayley Lock studied fine art textiles at Goldsmiths, University of London in the UK. She now lives in Suffolk where she works as an artist and lecturer. Hayley creates 2D and 3D structures using drawing, collage, painting, and sculpture. Her work is inspired by misconstrued snippets of conversation, music, memories, curiosities, folklore, portraits, and dark secrets. Her work has been exhibited widely within the UK.

1 The images in this piece have been digitally manipulated and then collaged together using a range of low- and high-tech materials, including Fabriano paper, stickers, ink, glitter, and glue. Hayley takes her inspiration from folklore and Swedish painting and portraiture.
2 Taking the media and celebrity as her inspiration, Sarah digitally manipulated a Dutch Masters portrait and then collaged onto Fabriano paper with stickers, sequins, and glitter.
3 This piece was collaged using paper, stickers, ink, glitter, sequins, fringing, and beading. Influenced by the sideshow, the fringing hides the character's face and creates a sense of curiosity.

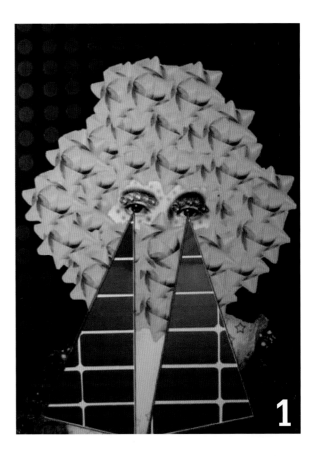

1

2

3

Martha Rich

Martha Rich lives in Pasadena, California, and works as an artist and part-time teacher. Martha began her career working in corporate America, but after becoming disillusioned took an evening art class run by the Clayton Brothers (established and widely exhibited painters). They immediately saw potential in her work and encouraged her to quit her corporate job—something she has never looked back on. Martha mainly works in acrylic and collage, and her career highlight has so far included painting murals for Beck's "Girl" music video. Murphy Design have also published her book, *Freedom Wigs: Sketchbook Expressionism & Other Personal Things.*

1–5 Pages from Martha's sketchbooks, which are full of self-initiated collages made with imagery from old food magazines combined with acrylic paint, type, and hand-drawn elements.

1

2

3

Jodie Hurt

Jodie Hurt studied art education at the University of Missouri, and lives in Kansas City where she works as an art educator. Jodie has been creating ever since she could hold a crayon. However, it was starting an Etsy online store that helped her to develop and define her work. Vintage ephemera, modern design, and antique photographs and books are Jodie's main inspirations, and she enjoys taking these sensibilities and turning them into something new.

1–6 This series of inventory tags was made by collaging vintage ephemera, scrapbooking paper, graph paper, origami paper, clip-art images, Gocco prints, and paint swatches. Jodie incorporates bold colors in her work and enjoys composing images in interesting and unexpected ways.

4

5

6

MIXED-MEDIA WALL ART:
Hollie Chastain

For this piece of wall art I have chosen to use a background made from the pages of an old geography book. The edges and colors on the page were so beautiful, and I knew straight away that I wanted to make something with it. I love the use of subtle textures in collage. For this piece I decided I wanted to use two house-like structures, and everything grew from there. I stumbled into a biology theme after finding the skull in another textbook. With this project, the creative inspiration came from the piece itself as it was coming together.

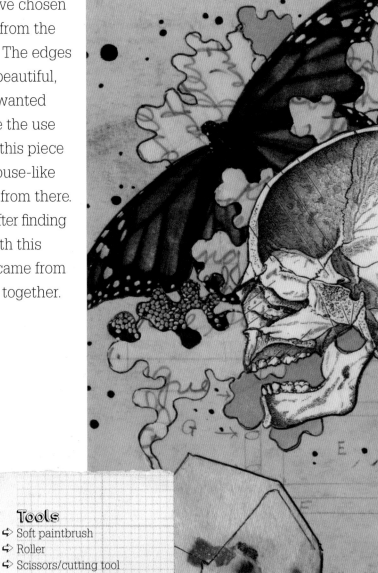

Materials
- ➪ Various paper samples
- ➪ Wood panel
- ➪ Adhesive
- ➪ Tracing paper
- ➪ Pencil
- ➪ Glue
- ➪ Marker pens
- ➪ India ink
- ➪ Clear spray gloss

Tools
- ➪ Soft paintbrush
- ➪ Roller
- ➪ Scissors/cutting tool

01 I start every project with a vague idea of what I want to produce, and then choose a background that I want to work on. Sometimes I use book covers or interesting pieces of paper mounted on a wood panel. You can get wood panels from art and hardware stores, or you can make your own. If you use the back of a picture frame as your panel then your piece will be ready to hang once it's sealed.

02 Once you have chosen your main materials, have a look through some paper samples and pick out a piece that you want to use. This step also helps your idea to develop. I tend to choose paper samples that work well together but have enough contrast to produce an interesting end piece.

03 The next step is to stick the paper onto the wooden panel. There are many adhesives you can use (I like Mod Podge because it seems to be the most user-friendly). Apply an even layer to the wooden surface with a soft paintbrush and place the paper down in position. A rubber roller is great for getting rid of bubbles and ripples that can pop up, so roll this over the paper to smooth it out.

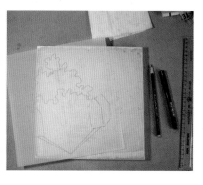

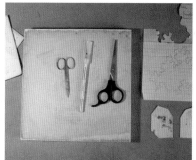

04 Use a piece of tracing paper to work out a plan and develop a design around any interesting aspects of the background that you don't want to cover up.

05 Once you have a few ideas for your base layer, cut out some shapes from the paper samples. I usually cut out more than I need so that I have plenty of options when I start to place and move things around. You may need to use different cutting tools according to the paper, but after a while you will learn what works best.

06 Once all of the pieces have been cut out, place them down on the paper. You may need to move things around before you're happy with the composition—it's sometimes a good idea to walk away and come back with a fresh perspective. I like to piece the entire collage together before the first piece is actually glued onto the background.

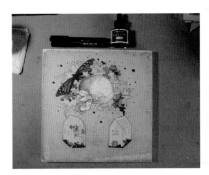

07 Once you're happy with the composition, glue the pieces down. Use a soft paintbrush to apply glue either onto the back of the piece or directly onto the canvas. Use the rubber roller after each adhesion to smooth out any wrinkles and make sure everything is attached.

08 Now it's time to add outlines. This is one of my favorite steps—there is something so satisfying about making each piece separate with a thin black outline. I like to use Faber-Castell's collection of PITT Artist Pens, which come in a variety of tips.

09 Ink details play a big role in many of my pieces— I love the texture it adds. In this step you can drop spots of black India ink onto the piece and fill in smaller spots with a pen if you want to be particular about placement.

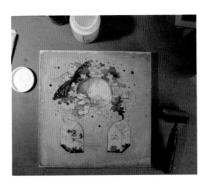

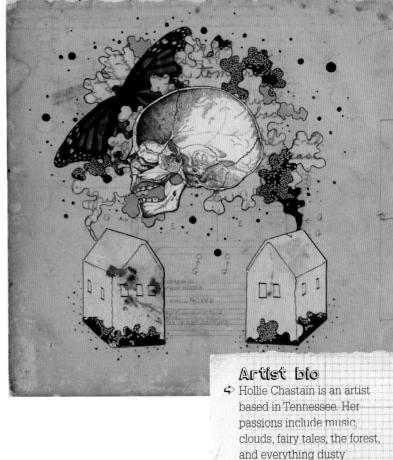

10 Once you're happy with the finished product it's time to seal! The sealant brings out the richness in the papers and darkens certain areas and edges. Use the same adhesive as in step 3 and carefully apply up to three coats across the surface of the collage with a paintbrush. Make sure the coat has completely dried before adding another, and try to keep the brush strokes well hidden.

11 After letting the sealant completely dry, add a hook to the back of the wood (if it needs one). Finally, spray on a coat of clear gloss (I use Krylon Preserve It!) and the piece is ready to hang!

Artist bio
↪ Hollie Chastain is an artist based in Tennessee. Her passions include music, clouds, fairy tales, the forest, and everything dusty and worn.

3D PHOTOGRAPHIC COLLAGE:
Sharon Wilson

Whenever I visit thrift stores I'm always drawn to boxes of old photographs and slides. After poring over these lost souvenirs and wondering who the people in the photographs are, I decided to bring them back to life and create new moments and memories. These "new moments in time" are collaged pieces of art that I hope evoke the same curiosity and interest I felt when I first discovered them. Reusing old slides and photographs brings a purpose and appreciation back to an otherwise obsolete object. The quality given by the film grain, dust, and scratches instantly makes these images appear as if they've come from a magical time far removed from today's digital age.

Materials
- Old slides or photographs
- Wooden box
- Primer
- Paint
- Ruler
- Acrylic mirror
- Spray adhesive
- ³⁄₁₆in (5mm) foamcore
- Hot glue
- Wood veneer

Hardware
- Computer
- Scanner
- Printer

Software
- Photoshop

Tools
- Hot glue gun
- Scissors
- Craft knife

01 Select some slides or photographs to use in your project. Look for elements that can be picked out easily and for interesting subjects that can be put together to build a fantastical scene. Landscape shots, for example, are great to use as background images. Even the most unassuming and boring photos can have gems hidden within them. If you want your collage to have a sense of reality, try and source your elements from similarly lit photographs.

02 Scan your images. Open the image you want to use for your background in Photoshop and scale it to the dimensions of the box or frame you are using.

03 Copy elements from other images and paste onto your background image to build up the collage, making sure that all of your pieces are pasted onto separate layers.

04 Arrange the pieces of your collage onto your main background image until you have a scene that you are happy with. If you want to give the image a cohesive appearance, play with the Image > Adjustment tools and alter the Color Balance and Brightness/Contrast levels so that all the pieces look as if they belong in the one photograph.

05 Separate your image into what will become the physical layers of the 3D collage. I am using 3⁄16in (5mm) foamcore to separate each layer and the box I'm using is 1in (25mm) deep, so I don't want to make more than five layers. Open a new Photoshop file and copy and paste your background into the new file. Go through your image, divide it into its physical layers, and paste them on layers in the new document. Look for natural horizon lines and outlines to determine the separations, keeping in mind that you don't want shapes that are too difficult to cut out with scissors.

06 Print out the individual layers. Use a heavy grade paper, as it will hold the shapes well.

07 Prepare the box for your collage. Any form of tray or frame can be used. You can add a coat of primer to the bottom to seal the wood and stop the paper from deteriorating. Paint the outside of the box a neutral color. These edges will not be very visible in the end, so there is no need to be too particular.

08 Measure the length and depth of the inside walls of the box and cut the acrylic mirror to these dimensions. Remember that the length of the short pieces of acrylic will be the inside wall length minus two times the thickness of the mirror. Hot glue the long pieces and then the short pieces to the inside walls of the box.

09 Measure the final internal dimension of the box and trim the printouts accordingly. Spray glue onto the background piece and stick it to the back wall of the box.

10 Cut strips of foamcore to fit the back of each layer. The more area that is covered by the foam, the sturdier the layer will be. Make sure that the pieces of foam are set back from the edge so that they will be hidden from the viewer. Hot glue the layers into the box in order. It's best to do a dry run first to make sure everything fits before gluing the pieces down.

11 To make the template for the wood veneer surround, draw two lines on a piece of card that are the same lengths as the inside measurements of your box. From the corners, draw 45° lines to the height that you would like the surround to be. Mark the centers and draw one half of the design. Cut the pieces out, fold in half, and trace and cut to complete your frame surround template. Use this to outline two long and two short pieces on the wood veneer. Using scissors or a craft knife, cut out the veneer and use hot glue to apply it to the top edge of the box. Finish off the veneer with oil or varnish.

Artist bio
↪ Sharon Wilson gained her love for designing and making from her mother. She has worked as a gallery manager in Auckland, New Zealand, since completing a degree in object design in 2006.

COLLAGE AND INK DRAWING:

Jim Butler

Most of my finished artworks begin with drawings that are made out on location in the urban environment. I see the built environment as being composed of chance elements (buildings, street furniture, cars, people, etc.) that have been temporarily placed together. The techniques I use—ink lines and collage—echo this temporary placement. In this sense, my drawings aren't simply graphic, but also somehow autobiographical; they are a record of the process of seeing and thinking. The elements within my collages, therefore, carry both historical and autobiographical elements.

Materials
↪ Pieces of paper
↪ Sketchbook
↪ Pencil
↪ Glue
↪ Twig or paintbrush
↪ Fountain pen

01 I continually collect pieces of paper for my collages, including tickets, stubs, envelopes, vouchers, magazine cutouts, etc. My primary concern is color, although I am also particularly drawn to typographic elements such as numbers and postage marks. These elements aren't necessarily collected with a particular project in mind.

02 I like to sort the pieces of paper by color and put them into small bags that I can take with me on location. Along with small bags of collage materials, I also take India ink, pencils, glue, and fountain pens. It's also a good idea to carry a few sketchbooks around. One can be for finished drawings and the others can be filled with collages of one or two elements that interest you. These drawings can then form the basis for any prints or other artworks you might undertake.

03 Composition is hugely important when drawing out on location. Take a step to one side and the elements will rearrange themselves. I often spend hours walking around looking at different compositions before deciding on one that I'm happy with. Because I tend to work with flat pieces of color, I usually try to add a sense of depth in the foreground by including elements such as lampposts, trash cans, and other street furniture.

06 Complete your drawing with any further fine details. I often like to complete my drawings by adding in transient figures using a fountain pen. These are drawn very quickly and the lightness of the line is used to suggest a less permanent presence than the solid India ink used in the rest of the drawing. (See final image opposite.)

04 Once you've decided on your location, start by loosely tearing a few pieces of paper and placing them on the page. Tear these pieces carefully to the desired scale and stick them down with glue. At this stage I tend to decide how much space I want to give to the collage elements, remembering that white space within a drawing is hugely important to the overall composition.

05 Once you're satisfied with the composition of the collage, draw elements from your scene over the top of the collage with India ink. I like to draw with a twig or the end of a paintbrush, as it produces heavy, bold lines that stand out well against the richness of the collaged elements. A twig or paintbrush end can also produce a variety of marks, many of which are uncontrolled.

Artist bio
⇨ Jim Butler is an artist, printmaker, and lecturer at Cambridge School of Art in the UK.

MIXED-MEDIA PHOTO COLLAGE: Chen Ying-Tzu (Hazen Chen)

I like visiting flea markets in search of old photos, books, and antiques, and using them as inspiration in my work. For this project I chose an image from a book by British photographer Bryn Campbell. I'm deeply touched by his work, which captures the innocence of children. I have taken one of his photographs as the basis for this collage, which creates a new and entirely different narrative.

Materials
⇨ Paper
⇨ Masking tape
⇨ Sketchbook or paper/card
⇨ Acrylic paint
⇨ Cutting tool or scissors
⇨ Fine-tip pen
⇨ Patterned fabric
⇨ Glue
⇨ Spray paint

Tools
⇨ Paintbrush
⇨ Scissors or cutting tool

Hardware
⇨ Computer
⇨ Printer

01 Begin by tearing some paper and cutting masking tape into small pieces. You can use most kinds of paper, but make sure it's not thin, as thin paper can tear easily during the collage process.

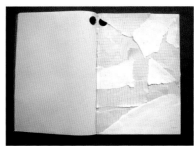

02 In order to prepare your background, arrange the torn pieces of paper in a notebook or on a piece of paper or card, and tape them down with the masking tape, filling in any vacant space. This will create a simple texture, and is an essential step in preparing your background.

03 Paint over your background with white acrylic and then paint over the white base with colored acrylics until the colors have combined.

04 Find an image that you want to use. I found this photograph in a book, but magazines and the internet are also good sources for finding interesting images.

05 Scan your image and make the alterations you require in Photoshop. In this instance, I have changed the image to sepia tone. Resize your image to the desired size and print a copy.

06 Choose the main element that you want in your collage and cut it out using scissors or a cutting tool.

07 Draw in further details by hand. Here I have added shadows on the fence using a black fine-tip pen in order to add a sense of depth.

08 This step involves adding some color to the characters. I have selected a piece of patterned fabric for the middle boy's shirt, cut it to size, and glued it in place onto the image. I have also added some color to the other boys' socks and shirt collars.

09 Cut out some words and glue them into place. I like to collect different flyers and adverts to use in my collages for this purpose.

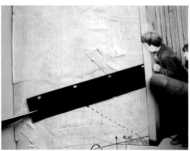

10 Now you can add in some further detail. I have drawn in technical line work in an attempt to connect the empty spaces with the images.

11 Glue in any additional elements. Here I have added some film negatives. For me, film negatives are effective as they add a really interesting element to the collage.

12 Now it's time to draw some of the finishing touches. Here I have added some speech bubbles using pencil, and then drawn over this with a black fine-tip pen to make them appear sharp and clear.

13 Once you're done, press lightly on the nozzle of a can of spray paint and spray a few drops onto the image.

14 If you want to make a digital version of your artwork, scan the collage and open it in Photoshop. Trim the size and adjust the brightness. Print out a copy and your collage is complete.

Artist bio
↪ Chen Ying-Tzu (Hazen Chen) is a graphic designer based in Taipei, Taiwan. More of her work can be seen on pages 146–147.

Contact Details

Able Parris:
ableparris.com

Anne Brassier:
airside.co.uk
airsideshop.com

Annika Koski:
kaniandesign.com

Ashley Thomas:
ashleythomas.webs.com

Bendita Gloria:
benditagloria.com

Bronwen Sleigh:
bronwensleigh.co.uk

Buff Monster:
buffmonster.com

Charlie and Sarah Adams:
charlieandsarah.com

Chen Ying-Tzu (Hazen Chen):
flickr.com/photos/hahahazen

Chrissie Abbott:
chrissieabbott.co.uk

Craig Atkinson:
craigatkinson.co.uk

Claudia Carieri:
claoodia.net

Dan McPharlin:
danmcpharlin.com

David Bradley:
davidbradley.jotta.com

Emily Robertson:
seeplats.com

Ethan Park:
ethanissweet.co.uk

Federico Martinez Aquino:
elfeder.com.ar

Gemma Anderson:
gemma-anderson.co.uk

Gluekit:
gluekit.com

Grady McFerrin:
gmillustration.com

Hardland Heartland:
hardlandheartland.com

Harmen Liemburg:
harmenliemburg.nl

Hayley Lock:
hayleylock.com

Hiutwig:
flickr.com/byhiutwig

Hollie Chastain:
holliechastain.com

Holly Wales:
eatjapanesefood.co.uk

Jon Burgerman:
jonburgerman.com

Jim Butler:
jimbutlerartist.com

Jacqueline Ford:
spagecko.wordpress.com

Jaco Haasbroek:
jacohaasbroek@gmail.com

Jenny Wilkinson:
jennywilkinson.com

Jesse Hora Dot Com:
jessehora.com

Jodie Hurt:
jodiehurt.etsy.com

Joe McLaren:
joemclaren.com

Kate Lyons:
iamkatelyons.co.uk

Kate Slater:
kateslaterillustration.com

Kenneth Do:
thegoodchild.com

Kipi Ka Popo:
kipikapopo.co.uk

Kirk Whayman:
kirkwhayman.com

Knit Sea:
knitsea.blogspot.com

Laura Jacometti:
jacomettidesign.com

Luisa Uribe:
luisauribe.com

Luke Best:
lukebest.com
peepshow.org.uk

Mack Manning:
memoryinlandscape.
blogspot.com
flomannuk@yahoo.co.uk

Marin van Uhm:
marinvanuhm.fr

Marion Lindsay:
d2454279.u51.surftown.se/
index.html

Martha Rich:
martharich.com
freedomwig.com

Matt Sewell:
mattsewell.co.uk

Mike Perry:
mikeperrystudio.com

Mithila Shafiq:
planetmithi.com

Modern Dog:
moderndog.com

Mysterious Al:
mysteriousal.com

Naomi Avsec:
ilovespoon.co.uk
naomiavsec.co.uk

Niessen & de Vries:
niessendevries.nl

Paul Willoughby:
paulwilloughby.com

Phil Barbato:
philbarbato.com

Pixelgarten:
pixelgarten.de

Robert Hope:
axisweb.org/artist/roberthope

Rui Tenreiro:
theculturefront.com

Sarah Keehan:
sarahkeehan.com

Sarah King:
sarahaking.com
eveningtweed.com

Sarah West:
sarahweststudio.com

Sharon Wilson:
pigeoncircus.com

Stanley Donwood:
slowlydownward.com

Susan Carey:
susancarey.com

Susann Stefanizen:
susannstefanizen.de

Will Hill:
will.hill@anglia.ac.uk

Your Secret Admiral:
yoursecretadmiral.com

Index

Acknowledgments

Thanks to Diane Leyman and Tony Seddon at RotoVision for their brilliant editorial support and art direction. Also to Will Hill for his recommendations and enthusiasm for the project, Christopher and Kathleen at Gluekit for their cover image and contributions, and finally to all of the contributors, with special thanks to those who created the many workthroughs throughout this book.